When I first came to Erik in 2019 our business was a bit of a mess and didn't have a clear vision. Within a year of working together, Erik helped us 7x our profit while simultaneously buying back a ton of our time by helping us implement a proven model and building micro teams. People like me pay Erik and Robby thousands of dollars monthly to help improve our business, yet in this book you will find many of the lessons these guys teach to their top coaching clients. Erik's become one of the most influential people in real estate and brings a huge vision to challenge the status quo that our industry has towards leading people and building teams. He has pioneered big solutions to common problems and has his fingerprints all over models such as the showing partner and ISA models. Erik is not a person that coaches on theory, he instead guides to what he has personally tried and tested within his own powerhouse team at Hatch Reality. Robby was one of the nations top ISAs before helping launch Hatch Coaching with Erik. He has reshaped and reframed the lead conversion space, creating multiple tech products that allow teams to scale their lead outreach and to connect with people on a human level, in addition to coaching many of the country's top ISA departments and rain makers. Having Erik in my corner not only massively improved our finances and our team, but also has made me a better husband, father and leader. Thank you Erik and Robby for your friendship, your leadership, and your massive contributions to challenging an industry that has a habit of being stuck in their old ways of thinking. Who would have thought that a couple of humble guys out of Fargo, ND would reshape the way leaders guide people and how real estate teams get built.

—Mike Novak
The Novak Team Brokered by Real

THE PERFECT REAL ESTATE AGENT BLUEPRINT

ERIK HATCH

ROBBY TREFETHREN

FREILING PUBLISHING

Copyright © 2022 by Erik Hatch and Robby Trefethren
First Paperback Edition

All rights reserved. No part of this publication may be reproduced, distributed, or transmitted in any form or by any means, including photocopying, recording, or other electronic or mechanical methods, without the prior written permission of the publisher, except in the case of brief quotations embodied in critical reviews and certain other noncommercial uses permitted by copyright law. For permission requests, write to the publisher, addressed "Attention: Permissions Coordinator," at the address below.

Some names, businesses, places, events, locales, incidents, and identifying details inside this book have been changed to protect the privacy of individuals.

Published by Freiling Publishing, a division of Freiling Agency, LLC.

P.O. Box 1264
Warrenton, VA 20188

www.FreilingPublishing.com

PB ISBN: 978-1-956267-62-4
e-Book ISBN: 978-1-956267-63-1

Printed in the United States of America

Table of Contents

Foreword vii
Introduction: A History of Hatch ix

Section 1
Understanding the Why

Chapter 1 Building Deep 3
Chapter 2 Get, Train, Retain 7
Chapter 3 Know Your Numbers 25
Chapter 4 How to Lead Yourself 33
Chapter 5 How to Lead Others 37
Chapter 6 Where to Get Business 41

Section 2
The Hatch Model Blueprint

Tier 1   The New Agent 57
Tier 2   The One (Wo)Man Band 61
Tier 3   Hiring Your First Admin 64
Tier 4   Hiring Your Second Admin 67
Tier 5   A Crossroads 70
Tier 6   Adding an ISA 82
Tier 7   Choosing Team Size 89
Tier 8   Development and Duplication 99
Tier 9   Mastering the C-Suite 105
Tier 10 Stepping Away 110

References 115

Foreword

As the co-founder and CEO of one of the fastest growing, publicly traded real estate companies in the world, I am blessed with the opportunity to meet the brightest people in this amazing industry.

Real estate is the single largest asset class in the world. As such, it attracts the brightest and most talented individuals. This industry caters to the very basic needs of us humans – the need for shelter, the need for a warm place to call home, and the need for a place to grow our family in. It revolves around money and emotions.

Throughout my life as a soldier in the special forces, a young student, and later as the CEO of several companies, I perfected the art of reading people. Business is all about people, and while I'm not a glorified manager nor am I an extraordinarily educated manager, I mastered the art of people.

In my 18 years in real estate, I had the privilege to work with and the opportunity to speak with thousands of real estate professionals and agents, from the newly licensed to the most successful team leaders and broker owners in the industry.

Erik Hatch and Robby T. stand out. They are two of the biggest names in our industry. When they speak, I listen. Through years of hard work of changing people's lives and cultivating success, they managed to create a brand and reputation for themselves.

I first met this power couple when they came to visit me and my team in New York. The connection was instant. The wisdom and passion for helping others was clearly reflected in their eyes. One pandemic later, I sat for dinner with Erik, and he was open and honest enough to tell me his life story. Raw. Unfiltered. It takes courage and confidence to expose yourself in such a way. It also takes strength, determination, and wits to leverage a personal crisis to become a leader.

Robby, like Erik, has a fascinating life story – born into a hardworking, blue-collar family, growing up on the edge of poverty, and harnessing the power of love to create a different, better future for his family. The most profound change is the birth child of pain. Nothing forces you to commit to a deeper change than pain.

Pain is what builds successful people and businesses. Ask any entrepreneur and they will tell you great stories about struggles, loss, and perseverance. The brave ones will also show you their scars. For me, that's the story of Erik and Robby. A story about personal evolution, about change, and about building massive success by taking the long, hard road.

It is a story about values, strength, drive, empathy, and family. A story about money and emotions. It took me one look into their eyes to know who these outstanding men were.

This book is a window into two of real estate's greatest minds who many call "legends." For Erik and Robby, this is yet another way to help people and pass along knowledge. For you, it's an opportunity to change your life.

Enjoy.

Tamir Poleg
Co-Founder and CEO
Real Brokerage

Introduction

A History of Hatch

Wherever you are on this real estate business journey, I bet I've been there. I was a part-time agent who had no momentum and massive debt. I eventually found success as a part-time agent, then an agent on a team, then a part-time agent again for a time before becoming a full-time agent on my own. I hired my first admin and eventually started a team.

At that time, I found myself as the leader of the team and doing almost all of the work with the rest of my team providing lackluster results at best. My ego got huge. I got kicked out of my brokerage. All but two people on my team left me. I started over and made a terrible business decision by aligning with the wrong broker. I had to rebuild.

After a 3-month fight with the state of North Dakota, who argued that I had too many blemishes on my record to allow me to even sit for the broker's test, I finally won that opportunity, passed the test, and started my brokerage. I had worked with two independent brokerages and a franchise and lost $120k in unpaid commissions from a bad business decision in aligning with one of them. I knew I wanted to run my own brokerage.

So, I started to build my new team. I was producing 150 transactions a year myself then got out of production. I found success through others. We are now selling over 1,000 homes a year. I will have sold over 6,000 homes by the time this book is published. I have expanded to different markets and failed. I have expanded to different markets and succeeded. I now work about one day a week in this business. I've opened up ancillary businesses. Some failed. Others succeeded. I now coach people around the country. There are teams within teams developing within Hatch Realty. Recently, we once again joined a national brokerage, and that's my ride.

I would venture to bet that you may see your own story in parts of my own. You name the mistake, and I've probably made it. I've made bad business decisions, bad hires, bad expansion moves, and bad ancillary business moves. You name a bump in the road, I have probably had to crawl my way over a similar one. I have had to fire some of my best friends. I have had some people I love dearly walk out on me. I have been through it all.

The truth is I got into real estate because I was flat broke. Real estate was my way to make up for bad financial decisions. In 2006, my first year in real estate, I sold zero houses. It was a healthy market in 2006, so I didn't have an excuse. The reality is I was giving it part-time effort and getting even less than part-time results. I was failing. Thankfully in 2007, I gained some momentum, figuring out a little bit of what I was supposed to do and how I was supposed to do it. I sold my first home … ironically, to my ex-girlfriend. Friends, don't ever underestimate the power of your sphere.

I sold ten homes my second year of real estate. I was with a local mom-and-pop brokerage at the time, and though I didn't get much leverage or support, I got to sell houses with a buddy of mine. In 2008, my third year, I found myself getting even a little better at it and sold 12 homes that year. I sold a total of 22 homes in those first three years, no expert by any means, and I was trying to balance real estate, a full-time job in youth ministry at my church, side hustling as a weekend DJ at wedding dances, and teaching guitar lessons to make ends meet.

We all have seasons in our lives and this was my season of working really hard. I got married in 2006 to my wife Emily, who was and still is a devoted elementary school teacher. For those first few years of our marriage, I was working about 90-110 hours a week. It was completely daunting and mentally tasking, but it was necessary. I was hustling my way out of a huge financial hole I had dug for us.

I joined Keller Williams Realty in 2009, and it was an awesome move for me. I spent about six months as a solo agent before joining a team. I wanted more at-bats. I was starting to gain more confidence and thought the team could provide me with more of the leads and leverage. I wanted more time to go sell because that's what I was comfortable with at the time. That's what I was good at. I was slaying open houses and getting really good within my sphere so my conversion rates were strong. Traditional lead generation was never really my style. You wouldn't have found me hammering through old leads to call, but I did it in my own way, discovering my own niche and leaning on my own unique skill set. I found real success for the first time in real estate and managed to sell 15 homes in 2009 as a part-time agent.

Midway through 2010, after being with the team for about 12 months, I got a call from a guy named Doug. He said, "Young man, you don't know me, but you were the volunteer coach for my granddaughter's basketball team for the last couple years. Her name is Katelyn."

Of course, I remembered Katelyn. I was a volunteer basketball coach for the girls' 7th and 8th grade B team. These girls were the nicest kids on the planet, but they weren't all-star athletes compared to some of their peers. We may have snuck in a couple of wins here and there, but it was a mess most of the time. Doug was at those games. He watched the way I coached. I knew Katelyn was hearing impaired, so I took it upon myself as her coach to ensure things were as visual as possible so she didn't miss out.

"Look, there's a condo I want to buy, and I want your help," he said.

I was thrilled.

"Wow, Doug. That's incredible. When do you want to go see the condo?" I asked.

"Young man, you're not listening to me. I said there's a condo I want to buy. I already know the seller. I already know the price. I just want you to write it up for me and Sally, and I want you to have the commission," Doug explained.

I was stunned. In a 2010 Fargo market, I had been assuming this condo would be a 90k gem. But it was a 320k condo. I hadn't sold any homes in that price range at that point in my young career, and now I didn't even have to show it. It felt like it just dropped right into my lap, but that wasn't true. It was the product of investing my time and energy into my community for decades with no asking of anything in return.

I went to the owners of the real estate team around that same time and explained I had been getting a lot of my business from my own sphere. I was the top-selling agent on that team and had started to gain some major momentum. I also had listings coming in. My ask of the owners was to consider the possibility of me earning a higher percentage on my sphere deals and find a way to start adding on the listing side of things.

"Sorry, that's not how we're built," they said.

I probably would still be with that team had their answer been yes, but they gave me a flat-out NO instead. That NO was the water that helped grow my seed of confidence into a little tree. I knew it was time to branch out on my own. I saw my potential, found a rhythm, and believed in what I could do, and I got a NO.

The beauty in that NO is that it helped me develop one of my favorite business philosophies that drives me as a leader today. If someone were to come to me and say, "Erik, I want to make 100% commission on my transactions. I want to work two hours a week. I want your office. I want to have my cake and eat it too." I would never tell them **no**. They would get a, **YES!** followed by *when*.

By giving someone a "Yes, when …," we create a benchmark of opportunity and abundance we didn't have before. Had my team at the time told me, "Yes, when …" instead of no, I would have wanted to keep running with them. But I felt rejected, limited, and stuck, so I left.

I had gained the confidence and financial momentum to give me the gusto I needed. Real estate was about to unlock huge leadership growth for me and massive financial opportunities for my family.

It was at this same time that Emily and I were battling infertility. We started trying to get pregnant in 2008-2009. The "trying" was my favorite part, you know? But month after month, we would face the disappointment of negative pregnancy tests. We then attempted something known as IUI, intrauterine insemination, to increase the likelihood of a pregnancy. We tried various medical procedures over the course of two years, used up our insurance, and lived through the pain and torture of waiting and waiting. Still no baby.

I knew the only way I would become a dad … the only way I would get to watch Emily become a mom would be to self-finance it. On one hand, I have a ministry career that I love and am good at, but it barely pays the bills. On the other hand, there is this lucrative real estate career I've been using as a vehicle to dig myself out of a financial hole. I never loved real estate like I loved ministry. I know so little about houses, and I'm not handy by any means. Truthfully, I didn't even know sheetrock and drywall were the same thing until a couple of years ago. I felt I lacked the skills necessary to make this my full-time career.

In 2011, I switched from full-time ministry to full-time real estate with Keller Williams. Even though I had sold 24 homes in 2010 and was approaching six figures in real estate, I was still too afraid to live on commission alone, so I picked up a part-time position at North Dakota State University's Lutheran Center as the campus pastor. With more time to dedicate to my real estate business, I was gaining some incredible momentum.

I attended countless high school graduation open houses in May 2011, eating my fair share of pulled pork sandwiches and tacos-in-a-bag at each (true Midwest staples) and getting to celebrate milestones with some awesome kids. It was at one of those open houses that I ran into Mariah, one of my former youth ministry kids. She was home from Iowa State for the summer and looking for work. I hired her on the spot for $10/hour without a plan for what she would do or how it would work. And it was a mess.

Instead of assigning her jobs that would lighten my load a bit, I gave her all of my honey-do list projects. She focused on all of the new projects I had been thinking about but didn't have the time to execute. Mariah is an incredible lady, but she came into my world with no real estate knowledge or experience, so the work she was doing was adding more to my plate instead of taking things off of it. She was poorly trained, and I set myself up for failure. Hire #1? I failed her … and myself.

Mariah returned to college at the end of that messy summer, and I hired a lady named Kim, who has gone on to be a titan in the real estate industry. She is now a team leader with Keller Williams on the East Coast. Kim and I butted heads frequently for two main reasons – Kim wasn't designed to be an admin, and I wasn't designed to lead her at the time. I was trying to make it *The Erik Show*. We managed to make it through a year together.

By the end of 2011, my first year in real estate full time, I sold 52 houses. All 52 of those were either from my sphere, a referral, a past client, or somebody I met through an open house. By this time, I had stopped teaching guitar lessons and DJ-ing and was honing in on relationships and real estate. I made over $200k net profit that year. My expenses were minimal – office rent, admin salary, and my split to Keller Williams. The rest was profit, and that felt great.

I thought I was following all of the rules and finding success the right way, and I assumed the next right step was to build a team. Keller Williams offered classes on how to start a team, so I did my due diligence, took the classes, and felt confident that I knew who to hire and how to do it. But I was dead wrong, and that was the start of a long string of mistakes I would make over the coming months.

I started 2012 with a team of four – Kim, myself, and two others. By the end of February 2012, I had a team of eight. By the time summer hit, I had expanded into two markets – one 70 miles north of Fargo in a town called Grand Forks and the other five hours northwest in the oil patch of North Dakota in a town I had never even been to before. I expanded to commercial businesses in northwest North Dakota because incredibly lucrative commercial opportunities presented themselves – a fiberglass company at $8 million and a trucking company at $20 million landed on my plate. I had a team of 11 in Fargo and two in Grand Forks. By the end of 2012, we sold 192 homes in our first year as a team, yet I was responsible for 113 of those 192 transactions or six out of every ten homes, broken down more simply. That's a recipe for disaster and a weak team model.

I was a great salesperson and a terrible leader. There was one other agent on my team with a respectable 18 transactions that year, but truthfully, I was the only one finding great success. I was buying internet leads and throwing them at my agents. I was handing off some of my referrals and hoping it would work out. We would meet once a week to discuss numbers and stats, and it was just miserable. I was running a poorly functioning business because it wasn't about success through others – it was about success for me. I made a lot of money, and nobody else did. I had no idea what I was doing.

Three months later, I was in Minneapolis receiving an award for the Top Real Estate Team for the North Central Region, which spans six states. It was my first year leading a team, and we were being recognized as the top team in the upper-midwest. My ego was through-the-roof **enormous**. I got back to Fargo, and suddenly I was being booked for speaking gigs. I was booked for three Keller Williams speaking events the week before Easter, so I headed back to Minneapolis. I spoke at three Keller Williams offices and felt confident that all went well. After the final event, I went out with folks from the market center and their team leader/good buddy of mine, Kent.

I got a call from my broker in Fargo while we were out. I answered the call and heard words that made my stomach drop.

"Erik, what did you do?," she asked nervously.

I had no idea what she was talking about, so she filled me in. There was an agent on my team who was licensed in Minnesota, and though Minnesota and North Dakota are reciprocal states, this agent couldn't get licensed in North Dakota due to a blemish on his record. That much I knew, but she went on to explain that this agent improperly represented themselves in a transaction. She explained this was a transaction I had signed off on.

I messed up and did so in a big way. I was moving so fast and undertraining so badly that I wasn't even aware my agent was misrepresenting himself. I carelessly signed off on something without even batting an eye. The day after Easter, I went into the office and was shown the door. I was fired, but somehow, I was still convinced my crap didn't stink. I thought to myself, *This Keller Williams office must be so stupid. How in the world could they let go of someone as valuable as me? They are going to fall apart without me. They're the problem, not me.*

I invited my whole team over to my home the next morning and tearfully explained to them what happened. I also let them in on my grand plan. I had already lined up a couple of offices and brokerages for us to consider. We went to check them out then returned to my house to debrief. I had thrown in the whole "hope you will make this transition with me" for good measure but felt so confident about this team. *They wouldn't leave me.*

But once again, I was dead wrong. All but two of them fired me on the spot. I was the problem, but I was too arrogant to see it right away. And slowly discovering that was one of the hardest realities I've had to face. I had fumbled in a big way and was more of a liability than an asset. I lost some really close friends in the process of losing my team and had to stand in the truth that I had really let people down.

In addition to the three remaining members of my team, myself included, I had two more people set to join the team. I called both of them and informed them about the situation, allowing them the option to make an informed choice for themselves about what was best for them. I explained that I truly believed this next place would be a good landing spot for us, and I still wanted them to work alongside me. They both made a pretty incredible investment in me by saying yes – they still wanted to join the team.

I was initially relieved but soon realized the heavy repercussions of my blunder. There might as well be a scarlet letter on my forehead in real estate circles. The real estate circle in a small town like Fargo can be incredibly gossipy and short-sighted. That gossip really ate at my confidence. I felt plagued, like everything I touched would turn to garbage. I felt like a failure.

I needed a fresh start. Maybe the real estate community wouldn't give it to me, but I could give it to myself. I chose to recommit to this profession with a new vision. It had been *The Erik Show* my first go-round, and we all saw how that turned out. So, now it was time to help others find success. I needed to make sure that every single one of my team members became a superstar in their careers.

All of a sudden, this felt aligned with my strengths in ministry. I knew that if I could help these people create big lives, that would be true success. I became diligent in my hiring process to make sure I was hiring the right people for the right positions. I became even more diligent in my training process to ensure I was teeing people up for the most opportunity possible. I was pouring the best of myself into this business, working 120+ hours a week. I was sleeping about four hours a night, working from sunup to sundown.

God bless my wife for going through that chapter with the grace she did. It was during this same period of time that we suffered three miscarriages and an ectopic pregnancy. We were more defeated than we had ever been, and it felt like all we had was each other. I was throwing myself into work for two reasons at that time – 1) to avoid the pain of not having a baby to hold, and 2) trying to change the stars and set us up for the day we may finally be able to start our family.

I had started 2013 growing a team of 13 people which shrunk to three and then grew to nine people by the time 2013 came to a close. We sold 246 homes that year. I was responsible for 153 of those. I did that while rebuilding, rebranding, getting my broker's license, opening our new Hatch Realty office, hiring new staff, and getting our systems going. I didn't have a showing partner. I didn't have DocuSign to help simplify things. This stage was done by the good old-fashioned grind of the business, and the momentum created was tremendous.

We opened Hatch Realty in January 2014 and let go of what I refer to as our rebound girlfriend brokerage. I had learned some hard lessons and needed to have control of my business. I needed to jerk that steering wheel onto my own path, and our rebound brokerage wasn't happy about it. They knew they would be a short-lived transition for us, but they didn't know just how short. They felt I needed to pay for the way I treated them.

Hindsight is 20/20, and there are things I would do differently now. But ultimately, I acted within legal and ethical bounds and brought in some great business for them. I truly believed I acted in goodwill, but to them, it felt as if I gave a big middle finger on the way out. That demonstrates the importance of perspective, and they stuck it to me with $120k of unpaid commissions.

I had just purchased our new office and was a hair away from bankruptcy for the second time in my life, the first of which led me to real estate in the first place. I remember talking to my coach at the time, a man named Steve Kout, and telling him I was terrified that I was about to lose everything. I'll never forget what he told me.

"Erik, you have the right to sit on your pity pot right now. Go ahead and sulk and wallow and say this is unfair. Stay there as long as you want, but then you need to make a decision to be the leader your team needs right now. You need to decide how long you're going to wallow because they need you to lead. Go lead your team like you're called to do," Steve said.

So, I gave myself one last night to feel bad for myself.

And when I woke up the next day, I made the decision to move forward. I fired up the troops and added two more to our team right at the start of the year, taking us to 11 total. We grew to 19 members by year's end and sold 411 houses.

I hired our first ISA (inside sales agent), Josh Boschee, in 2013, and hired our second with the addition of Robby Trefethren at the end of the year. We started our showing partner model by adding Connor Johnson and Lucas Paper in the summer of 2014. We were changing the way real estate was done. We were training, practicing, and role playing together every single day. I still sold 149 homes myself, but for the first time in my career, my team was producing more than me. We were finally starting to figure this thing out. We were creating an environment rich in the kind of culture and character that made people want to stick around. It was so much fun.

My brokerage business was born in January 2014, and it filled me with a pride I had never felt before. Then October of that same year brought an even greater joy that changed my entire world. After years of infertility, pain, and struggle, Emily and I finally welcomed our daughter Finley into the world. Within that one year, I became the business person, man, and father I had longed to be for so long. I decided right then and there to get out of production. Nearly 150 transactions for two straight years, and I was going to be done. I may have done a couple dozen that next year, but by and large, my production days were over.

Everything kept rocking and rolling at Hatch Realty. We went from **411** transactions in 2014, to **516** in 2015, then to **592** in 2016. We sold over **600** homes in each of the three years after that, **866** homes in 2020, and **1,023** in 2021.

Let's break down just how that growth happened after my exit from production in 2014. At the end of 2014, we were a team of 19. We are now standing strong with 55 people and counting as we write this book. We have expanded into three other markets - Bismarck, Grand Forks, and Minnesota lakes country. There are 19 people on the team who managed to make over $100k in 2021, which is an absolutely incredible thing to stop and think about. Four people made over $400k.

Perhaps most importantly, we have managed to retain a great deal of talent in recent years, despite painful bumps along the way. There was a time in 2018-19 that this company hated me. We were going through a lot of turmoil. Our company was becoming something it wasn't designed to be, and we made a lot of mistakes. We lost a lot of people. Some were fired. Some quit. But each one hurt. I was so emotionally wrecked by some of those exits and so close to burnout that giving it all up crossed my mind more than once. I can't disclose the details of those issues out of respect for the privacy of those involved, but I want to stress that we walked through some major fires together. I'm proud to say we've come out stronger because of it, and we have lost only a couple of producers in the last three years.

To grow a great business is one thing, but to maintain a great business is something else entirely. Keeping great people around will be one of the hardest things you ever do. It was only through the intentional development of people, particularly other leaders, that we at Hatch Realty got back on track. Our saving grace came in the form of a massive amount of dedication by people who truly care.

As a leader, it can often feel like one wrong move will lead to great people walking out the door. I used to be really afraid of that, but I'm not afraid of it anymore. I've seen some really hard days over the last decade, and I'm really comfortable with **who I am now** and **who God called me to be**. I am confident God is allowing me to use my business as a ministry to reach people and make a tangible difference in this world. I have created a repeatable, duplicatable system that is built on a next man- or woman-up mentality. If people want to leave, which they have and they will, then we have some well-trained next-up troops. We will certainly miss those we poured into, but we won't miss a beat as a company.

I have gradually spent less and less time in the business of Hatch Realty over the last seven years. This was only possible through the intentional development of other leaders. I started that transition with a group of people who really served like a group of consultants for me. They would inform me of what was going on within their departments and then would **watch me** make decisions. I would use their insights to make those decisions and would explain to them why I was making those decisions, but ultimately, I still held the reins. That leadership group then moved into the **watch you** portion of development, where they were the ones leading the conversations and brainstorming solutions, and I was there as a consultant, providing feedback and suggestions but allowing them the chance to lead.

How to Train and Empower Your Team

1. WATCH ME
Shadowing is essential for the new person to see you in action.

2. WATCH YOU
This is oftentimes the most skipped over piece and yet the most important – taking the time to shadow the new person is a cornerstone for success. Do not skip this step! Don't leave this step too quickly, either. A lot of coaching and accountability exists here.

3. GO AND DO
Once they've watched you and you've seen them perform well, they have now earned the right to own the role.

The final stage, where that group continues to function today, is **go do**. I am currently running a nearly $8 million company and doing so working at that business only one day a week. Those leaders have the talent and capacity to make the decisions without feeling obligated to seek my approval or oversight. They represent the best interests of their departments and make nearly every decision without me. Sometimes, I'm there as the crotchety old man, telling them how I think things should be done, but I mostly try to stay quiet. I want to allow them the freedom and the ability to step into those leadership roles without me breathing down their necks.

I have been spending more of my time with Hatch Coaching these days. At this point in my career, I feel called to make an impact and influence this industry and become the most influential person in our real estate sandbox. I plan to do that in three ways. First, I have to nurture an exceedingly healthy team at Hatch Realty. Second, I have to be a strong voice in this industry, along with my coaching partner Robby T. We have the opportunity to make a deep impact on the people we get to work with and influence. Lastly, our recent partnership with Real Brokerage has allowed us the chance to join a group of people who are rowing this boat together. We are aligned in mission and values. It is one of the most exciting experiences of my career thus far.

I originally jumped into real estate full time over a decade ago for what I thought would be a short time until I found my next calling in ministry. I was planning to make some money, right some wrongs, then jump ship. But the beautiful thing that unfolded is this career actually transformed into my ministry. Hatch Realty is now the vehicle through which many other dreams have been realized - mine included. Wherever you are on your real estate journey, whether you're running a small business of three or four people, working as a part-time agent, thinking about leaving the business entirely, or leading a massive company, I've been there.

This book will serve as a guiding tool to walk you through whatever you need to in order to find your calling in real estate. This book will help you hone in on your purpose and your plan to best serve your clients, your team, your family, yourself, and your own capacities. This world and this industry doesn't need more realtors, but we could all use more servant-hearted leaders. When we can do that, I have the utmost confidence in the future of real estate.

So, as you dive into this blueprint of how to build the perfect real estate business, you get to choose your adventure. If you want to go big, we have you. If you want to stay small but mighty, we have you. If you need to get your numbers right, we have you.

Robby T and I have poured our experiences and perspectives as both players and coaches to help you build the perfect business. You'll get the chance to dive into all of the details followed by a step-by-step blueprint to guide you as you grow. And we're confident that the industry's traditional models won't get you the magnificent life you long for. Our model will.

We have you.

Erik Hatch

1 Understanding the Why

Chapter 1

Building Deep

There's a giant threat to y'all's real estate businesses, and you're about to be broke and miserable. The game is changing, and we all need to change too if we want to stay afloat. Technology certainly captures consumers' attention at a high level, but it also puts real estate businesses in a financial squeeze. Other models and coaching companies will attempt to throw Band-Aids at broken arms, telling you, *"Just hire more!"* But **more people will not necessarily get you more results** - at least not in a sustainable way.

So, you're left with a couple of options if you want to win in the modern real estate game. You either need to win the technology game which I highly doubt any one of us is going to do given the ever-changing and evolving world of tech or the other option which is not only more feasible but far more accessible, winning the relationship game. We, as an industry, have been trying to figure out how to script people and build models which do make great money but continually miss the mark. If you're not a great person and if you don't make people feel unbelievable, then it's all smoke and mirrors. Real estate businesses are focusing on what can cash out today instead of building a model that'll be strong well into the future.

We have noticed that many teams selling over 300 homes annually are profiting less than a 10% profit margin, if not a net negative when their numbers are done correctly (which we will discuss in Chapter 3). We see they are often getting poor conversion rates out of new and/or mediocre talent and keeping their business afloat with their own personal production. These leaders may call it team profit when in actuality it is their own production keeping the business afloat.

At Hatch Realty, we observed a ridiculous amount of value coming from seasoned agents. We knew we needed a system to help coach the rookie agents in a way that would lead to the same kind of success, and we noticed something really interesting when we really took a look at the numbers. A first-year agent who started off in production, not as a showing partner (a role we will discuss in depth later in the book), converted on average 16% of their appointments into closings. First-year agents in production who started off as a showing partner converted at an average of 31% their first year in production - nearly double what someone newly recruited into the agent role could convert.

That in and of itself could be the sole argument for the showing partner model (which we will discuss in Tier 5 of Section 2), but wait, there's more! Second-year agents in production are averaging 28% conversion of company appointments. Agents who have been with us 3+ years are averaging 36% conversion. *(Note: Agents who have been in the business more than a year have the advantage of last year's appointments who have not yet converted.)*

Simply put, a team should value seasoned talent. It is financially irresponsible to give the same at-bats to new people and veteran agents. Finally, leveraging your top producers with a showing partner makes sense financially. It breeds investment into your valued talent, and it sets up the new hire to get their MBA in real estate before they ever have to "try" to make it as a producer.

Hatch Realty Conversion Numbers of Company Appointments:

(Measuring appointment set to closed transaction)
- 1st-year agents - 16%
- 1st-year agents (who start as a showing partner before they get into production) - 31%

- 2nd-year agent - 28%

- 3rd-year+ agent - 34%

*Don't expect the same production from agents on different rungs of the ladder!

It is an expectation in our world that an agent should be converting 18% of their first-year appointments, 28% their second year, and 36% their third year. But this is something that needs to be systemized and monitored every step of the way. We noticed something called **destructive abundance** occurring if there is not clear accountability and supervision throughout this process. If team members are overfed with too many leads or too many appointments, it leads to poor results. It's with that in mind that we say an agent shouldn't have more than 100 appointments set in a year. If they have a showing partner, that can go up to about 150 appointments at most, and there should be an increase of conversion with that partner on board, no matter what.

The reason we are writing this book is because we see the flaws in our industry, but we also know there is a way to pivot toward something better for you, your team, and your clients. When I say you're about to be broke and miserable, I mean we need to stop with the Band-Aids and actually heal the broken bone. We need to go deeper. We need a different, healthier approach. The last thing this industry needs is more wide teams full of mediocre players.

It's crucial to the success and sustainability of our teams that we **build deep first**. I'm convinced that the only way to stay relevant and deliver at a high level of service is with the best team and the best relationships. Buyers and sellers demand and deserve that kind of excellence, and the best way to get there is with a team full of excellent people. A real estate license isn't enough. That just tells me you took a class and passed a test. That's not excellence.

Excellent teams need to be carefully curated. Excellence requires that you hire with intention, train with meticulous dedication and vision, and continue to pour into people over time by providing an abundance of mentorship and possibility. One of my real estate role models, Ben Kinney, says that if you want to have Navy Seals, you first have to have a Navy. He's absolutely right. Once you identify your talent, it's imperative you run toward them with a sea of opportunity and growth. As you add more people to your organization, you need to build leverage around your Navy Seals by having new people train under them and work their way up. **Everything is earned, and nothing is given.**

HATCH HINT

Don't Forget

Everything is earned, and nothing is given.

Giving somebody an at-bat and an opportunity is good, but giving somebody a customized journey to achieve their dreams is great. We at Hatch not only want greatness, but we also want to **retain greatness.** There are a variety of reasons people leave real estate teams. Sometimes, the leadership sucks, they're not getting enough leads, or they're starting to produce more and feel they'd be better off on their own. But ultimately, what we've seen happen more than anything is quality agents leaving real estate teams because they've run out of opportunities to grow in that company.

I've been that agent who left because I ran out of runway. I left a team, not because I didn't care about them but because my future felt limited in that environment. Our goal at Hatch is to provide so much vision, leadership, culture, and opportunity that quality agents don't feel the need to leave to continue their growth. In fact, they feel their greatest growth and evolution will happen right here alongside us, and there is no place they'd rather be.

Now let's be clear - there's nothing wrong with building wide. In fact, we at Hatch fully endorse the idea of building wide and adding agents when a team is ready. But it is the depth of a team that matters most. We need to be **remarkable** in order to out-relationship the rest. You could build a wide team full of talented agents, but if you don't value relationships while creating a strong foundation of respect, honesty, compassion, and accountability, then you are building on shaky ground, my friends.

Robby Trefethren and I, having sold over 6,000 homes together and coaching some of the top real estate teams in the country over the last six years, are poised and positioned to help solve this problem. We know that building a deep business is a solution bursting with opportunity, not only for the rainmaker but for each individual team member. It's through people that you are going to find true and sustainable success. If you want to go fast, go alone. But if you want to go far, go together. And therein lies an amazingly fruitful opportunity.

Let's imagine we have two stables. One is filled with race horses, and the other is filled with donkeys. You put a couple of donkeys in with the race horses, and those donkeys are going to run faster than they ever have before. You put a couple of race horses in with the donkeys? There's a good chance those race horses are going to be acting like asses in no time. Our stables, our ecosystems, our businesses - they matter. The community we put people into matters.

If you want an unbelievable real estate business, you need to build a stable full of race horses. You need more race horses than donkeys, more Navy Seals than Reserves, more A-players than B-players, and more rock stars than mediocre talent show acts. You need greatness. And the only way greatness will stick around is if you build **a customized plan with an unlimited runway and massive proximity to great leadership.**

Race Horses and Donkeys

- You can put a donkey or two in a stable filled with race horses, and those donkeys will run faster than they ever have.

- You can put a race horse or two in a stable filled with donkeys, and those race horses will quickly resemble the asses they surround themselves with.

Chapter 2
Get, Train, Retain

What's the most important thing to do when leading a team?

1. **GET great talent.**
   Everything is easier with the right people. Everything.
2. **TRAIN great talent.**
   Helping these team members be their best selves is the greatest thing you can do for them (and your organization).
3. **RETAIN great talent.**
   Having an ecosystem and culture that is customized and provides opportunities for each person's continued growth is essential.

GET: PART 1 - PLAN WITH PRINCIPLES

Hiring great people into your ecosystem is simple, but it's not easy. There is a scene in the movie *Caddyshack* where the caddies go to the pool. One of the caddies throws a Baby Ruth candy bar into the pool, and people start running frantically (and hilariously) from the pool. Who could blame them? It looks like a giant turd in the water. A bad hire is a turd in the waters of your company. People will see that turd and want to stay far away from it. They may even lose trust in you, questioning why you'd ever allow that into the pool.

There has been a common theme in business to hire fast and fire fast. There's a fear that great talent will go elsewhere if they're not snatched up quickly, but we believe the opposite to be true. It is crucial to **hire slow and fire slow**. In fact, that is the first of our four core hiring principles.

To hire slow and fire slow means great leaders have to be 12 months ahead on vision casting and six months ahead on hiring. It means mediocre results are often a reflection of leadership. It means instead of punishing someone for falling short of expectations, we provide mentorship and support. It means there is a whole lot of accountability for those in leadership positions, which is an idea that makes many people uncomfortable. If someone is looking to grow, they also need to be okay with being uncomfortable. You will never get one without the other.

Leaders need to be far ahead with their vision!

A leader should be...
- 12 months ahead on vision casting
- 6 months ahead on hiring

The second principal is to **hire intentionally, not out of desperation.** You are not in the right headspace to hire intentionally if you are drowning in leads and everyone on your team is stretched thin. At that point, you just want a warm body in there to lighten the load. You may resort to hiring friends or hand-raisers. You'll choose the easy hire, but that's setting yourself up to fail in the long run.

Now you may be asking yourself, "Should I be hiring …?", and if you are, then you are probably already three months behind. But don't take that as us saying you should speed up. We want you to slow down. Delayed gratification is key in hiring the right people for your team. Let's imagine you have a licensed agent apply for a position. He's a pretty middle-of-the-road guy, likable enough, talented enough, but nothing spectacular. But you also have an insanely talented but unlicensed woman apply who is full of potential and possibilities. Between the hiring, licensing, and onboarding process, she isn't going to be working as an agent for six months or so. You may be tempted to go with the first guy, but she is the one you need to hire. We want to emphasize that delayed gratification for an insanely talented person is always worth it.

From this point forward, we want you to commit to being six months ahead on hiring so you can have people on the team before you need them. But we know taking on that kind of financial risk before you feel the necessity of it can be really scary. That's why you need to be vision casting 12 months ahead, planning and preparing for what you will need. You need to zoom out and see the big picture to know what comes next and why.

The third principle is to **hire people who naturally want to work in the role**. This sounds ridiculously simple, but it's not easy. The people you hire need to be a natural fit for the position they're in. If it goes against their natural tendencies, it's going to be a huge ask of them to adjust their general nature every single day. Let's take the agent role as an example.

Let's imagine you hire someone to be an agent who is incredibly introverted and lacks social savvy but absolutely loves houses. She loves HGTV. She doesn't necessarily love working with people, but she adores Chip and Joanna Gaines. That's not going to work, folks.

Agents work with people all day every day. It's important to find outgoing agents who can roll with the punches, or it will be asking a square peg to fit in a round hole each and every time they show up to work. That's not fair to them, and it's not fair to the team. We've also started coaching our clients to add a spouse/partner dinner to the hiring process for full transparency when adding an agent or ISA, saying something like, "In this new position, Jess is going to be working a lot of evenings and weekends. How do you feel about that?"

We want to make sure everyone is fully aware of the commitment they're making when they sign on to our teams. Agents and ISAs are also not traditional 9-5 positions, so it's also crucial they know what they're getting into from the start. If they are not aligned with this nontraditional lifestyle or if their spouse or partner isn't bought-in to the idea, it's not going to work.

The fourth principle is to **seek authenticity.** It's natural for someone to show up to a job interview with their best face forward, highlighting strengths and minimizing weaknesses. But one of the biggest dangers in hiring is taking someone at face value when your instincts are telling you that person is not being authentic to who they truly are. It is important to learn who people are at their core, and in order to do that, you need a thoughtful and intentional hiring process. When you go fast, you stay on the surface. But when you go slow, you can get to the deeper truth. *Who are they? Are they telling the truth? Are they being authentic?* When you take your time, you're able to spot who would be that turd-shaped candy bar in your pool and filter them out.

A key to finding and attracting the right people for your pool is **strategy**. One strategy we've adopted at Hatch is to avoid part-time hires. You may get a great part-timer, but if you want full-time results, you need to hire someone full time.

Part-Time Hires

- Part-time hires get you part-time results.

- If, by chance, they're great, your business will grow, but they have already signed up for partial commitment. You'll either need to replace them or grow only as much as their part-time schedule will allow.

- Whenever possible, hire someone full time.

We also take a three-pronged approach to hiring: advertise the listing, attract people through social media, and recruit people who would be a good fit. Though we will always post online ads for positions, it's not our only strategy. There are a lot of great people out there looking for jobs, so I say this with trepidation. However, we often find people looking at online job postings are miserable in their current positions. Sometimes, that misery is truly due to circumstances beyond their control - subpar management, poor ethics, toxic company culture, etc., but it is equally plausible that the person is in misery due to their own making.

We sometimes see these applicants, the ones running from a job that was "miserable," have a victim mindset and are in misery of their own making. They may be blind to their part in the dysfunction and dissatisfaction. Worse yet, they're not ready or willing to take responsibility for it. **They are running from something more than they're running toward something.** We want to find people who are running toward our company with the right motivation to better their lives.

Why are you looking to make a move?

You're either running FROM something or TOWARD something.

If you're running FROM something, often the next place you end up is an unintentional "rebound".

When you run toward something, you are pursuing the next best version of yourself.

There's nothing wrong with placing ads, but **recruitment is key.** You should do both. Talent is the number one way to change your ecosystem for the better. Talent can create systems, processes, and make the sales. Your job with good talent is to train them well then get out of their way. Robby T. was recruited to apply to Hatch as our second ever ISA by Josh Boschee, a story we will explain more in Chapter 4.

It's through that type of recruitment, trusted people vouching for someone with a stamp of approval to say, "They would be a great fit for us," that you'll find some of your very best talent. It's not only your team who can help in your recruitment efforts. Your spouse, your allies in the industry, your church friends, your social media community - all of them can help send the right people your way. To ensure you cast the largest net possible, **let your network know who you're looking for.** Post about it on social media, send the ad directly to people you hope will apply for it, and encourage others to share the news that you're hiring.

Social media is a tool in your belt, and it's **best to be showing, not just selling.** The best social media approach I can suggest is to be visible, not just for business. You can show how you treat your clients, how you treat your team members, what kind of opportunities are available in your company, and even what your family or close friends do to have fun together. People pay attention to stories. They don't care about information without a narrative. You may be posting every open house and every new listing, but if you're not also posting about stories and people, I can guarantee most people aren't even seeing your posts. Be consistent, tell stories, and have fun to increase your engagement and visibility.

HATCH HINT

3 Types of Recruitment

There are 3 ways in which people will seek you out to join your team.

1. Relationships
You have a personal connection to this person or a great referral source that tees you up for success.

2. Reputation
The likelihood for success is grand when someone sees who you are and seeks you out because of it.

3. Real estate
Those that love real estate as their primary catalyst for seeking you out often underperform or are flight risks. Their connection is to the job, not to you. Loving houses does not equate to being a stellar team member.

Relationships and reputation win the day!

Note: You can...reputation. It's simply harder to do.

GET: PART 2 - HIRING

The final piece to hiring the right people is being able to **play the long game**. Building a team of great people is more important to me than selling houses. My brand and reputation are crucial. If I want great people to come work at Hatch Realty, I've got to show up in the local community as a person worth following. I choose to be an active and engaged member of my community for many reasons, but the cherry on top is being able to create a wide network of great, talented people. Well over half of our team is made up of recruits and SOI (sphere of influence) from our existing team. Great people attract more great people.

Hatch Realty Nine Step Hiring Process

Step #1) **Place the right ad in the right place.**

We use a program called WizeHire which is essentially a top-notch CRM for hiring. Through WizeHire, we require applicants submit their application and resume, of course, but we also require they complete something called a DiSC assessment which allows us to see a general personality profile. We have found DiSC profiles to be an instrumental piece of our hiring process. WizeHire blasts out to other sites like Monster, Indeed, Craigslist, and LinkedIn without requiring you do those one-by-one. You can go to https://wizehire.com/hatch-coaching to learn more.

HATCH HINT

DISC Style: D is for Dominance
Personality Traits: Direct, demanding, driven, determined, developer, competitive, fast-paced, strong-willed, confident, creative
Values: Action, concrete results, freedom, challenges
Expends Energy: Patience, displaying sensitivity, looking at details
Communication Tips: Be focused, brief, and specific. Do not generalize or be repetitive. Focus on solutions.

HATCH HINT

DISC Style: I is for Influence
Personality Traits: Enthusiastic, warm, Impulsive, trusting, optimistic, collaborative, relational, affirming, promoter, persuader, appraiser
Values: Social recognition, counseling, freedom of expression, relationships
Expends Energy: Following through completely, researching all facts, speaking directly, staying focused
Communication Tips: Share your experiences. Give that person space to ask questions and talk. Don't overload on details. Don't interrupt.

DISC Style:	S is for Steadiness
Personality Traits:	Supportive, stable, calm, patient, predictable, deliberate, consistent
Values:	Loyalty, helping others, security, cooperation, sincere appreciation
Expends Energy:	Adapting to change, multitasking, promoting themselves, confrontation
Communication Tips:	Be personable and amiable. Express interest in them. Tell them what you expect from them. Be clear, polite, and gentle.

DISC Style:	C is for Conscientiousness
Personality Traits:	Careful, cautious, systematic, diplomatic, accurate, tactful, challenges assumptions, over critical, perfectionist, very analytical, fears criticism
Values:	Quality, accuracy, stability, systems, predictability
Expends Energy:	Delegating, giving up control, compromise, making quick decisions
Communication Tips:	Focus on facts and details. Minimize "pep talk" or emotional language. Be patient, persistent, and diplomatic.

Step #2) **Filter.**

Our hiring decision can be broken down into three categories. Culture makes up 50% of the hiring decision. Steps 3-9 will help to determine if the person is a cultural fit. The other two are 25% DiSC + values and 25% hunger.

DiSC makes up 25% because it gives us a window into who this person is at their core, how they work, and what they need to thrive. *Admin* should be a high S or C - the stabilizers and safety-oriented individuals. A high D score is not likely a good fit for an admin role. *Agent* should be a high I, love influencing and connecting with people. We often find that buyer agents are an I-S and listing agents are an I-D, but of course, that's just speaking in generalities. We avoid high Cs in agents because those cautious, detail-oriented, analytical folks are not the best fit for unpredictable, people-facing sales positions. *ISAs* are most commonly a high D or C. The ISA role is a data-based management ninja. D-S-C would be the ideal hire. High Is - 75% or higher - will not get their connection needs met in a role like this. There is a great deal of rejection and very little face-to-face contact.

The final 25% in our hiring decisions is gauging the level of a person's **hunger**. This is less important in an admin, but in terms of any sales-related position, hunger is an absolute must-have. But you won't necessarily find that on a resume. Hunger is a fairly loosely defined term, but we view it as the willingness to demonstrate how committed you are to something. **You can't teach hunger.** It is self-motivated. When does a person wake up in the morning? What books do they read? What podcasts do they listen to? What kind of people do they surround themselves with? How are you working to better yourself to change the stars for yourself?

It's important not to trust people for who they say they're going to be. **Trust who they are right now.** It's easy to commit to better habits tomorrow, next week, or next month because there's no accountability there. The things they are currently doing are far more important. It's the responsibility of the individual to build habits that demonstrate a hunger to be better. It's the responsibility of the leaders in an organization to find hungry people and help them harness that energy and channel it toward opportunities that will bring about a fruitful life for them and those around them.

Step #3) **Career Night**

Career night is the addition we put into our arsenal that truly changed the game. We placed an ad for my personal assistant a few years ago and got over 300 applicants. It took 10-15 hours just to read through the applications and filter through who may not be a great fit. We narrowed the list to anyone we wanted to get to know further and invited them to attend our Career Night. The beautiful thing about an event like this is it does a lot of the heavy lifting for you. Those individuals who were lackadaisical when looking for a job won't show up.

About 40 applicants took the initiative to show up for Career Night to learn more about the personal assistant position. We had about 55 "yes" responses for this particular event, but it is very typical for about 20-30% of those who RSVP "yes" to not show up. As the applicants came through the door, I was able to assess their nonverbals. I could see the way they carried themselves and the way they interacted with others. I got a real picture of the kind of person they were in new situations and what kind of energy they brought to a room.

Career Night is always awkward at the beginning. I like to lead a presentation focused on all of the reasons they may not want to work at Hatch Realty. If they expect it to be a smooth ride, anything that doesn't fit that narrative will lead to disappointment and anger. Unmet expectations are catalysts for unbridled frustration. We "set the stage" very intentionally. We want to undersell and overdeliver. We want to see who is still standing once we list off a myriad of reasons to second guess the opportunity.

Unmet Expectations

The biggest pain-points people experience in life are unmet expectations.

Over-communication is KEY! Set the stage for you to win in the beginning...every time.

In a sales role, we stress the intense hours and the fact they may not get paid for six+ months. Maybe they will be taking a pay cut. Maybe they will be stretched thin. There can be lawsuits involved. There will be angry clients, even when you've done nothing wrong. We name the pain points first so we can encourage them to take off the rose-colored glasses and see the role more realistically.

We then move into some of the highlights of the job, a question-and-answer time, and finally some face-to-face conversations with Hatch team members. Our Career Night events last anywhere from 60-90 minutes, but it is always time very well spent. In a matter of an hour and a half, I was able to narrow my personal assistant pool from 307 to six. I was able to assess who had the traits I was looking for and observe how they interacted, both individually and with the group. I was able to look for cultural fit and strengths they could bring to the organization. I was confident I would find who I was looking for in those remaining six. The next steps of our hiring process would help me do just that.

Step #4) **Ask essay questions.**

The morning after any Career Night, a series of essay questions are sent to applicants' inbox. For my personal assistant position, we sent the questions to all 55 of the applicants who RSVP-ed "yes," even if they ultimately did not attend. Perhaps they weren't able to make it due to unforeseeable circumstances, or perhaps social situations don't allow them to demonstrate their strengths, which is especially common for admin folks. These essay responses are an important piece of the hiring process because it allows people to shine in ways that maybe they didn't at Career Night. We set a deadline and allow only five days to respond. This allows ample time to craft thoughtful and thorough answers, if it is important to them. We got about 15-20 responses for this particular position.

We allow people to self-select out of the process by not responding or responding late. If someone is not willing to answer questions on time, they are not going to be a good fit for the position. Though we are not looking for perfect answers by any means, we are looking to get to know people on a deeper level. It is crucial that answers be coherent and easy to understand. If that's not something a person can do, they will not be able to survive in a world that constantly demands a great deal of written communication with teammates and clients alike.

Step #5) **Give a 30-minute interview (phone/in-person).**

This is a step most people have seen in action. In many organizations, the hiring team takes a look through applications, selects a few to interview, sets up and conducts interviews, then invites someone into their world. We clearly do things very differently. This is only step five of nine, after all.

The 30-minute interview isn't the final step before offering someone the position. Thirty minutes isn't nearly enough time to get to know someone well enough to invite them in. We're still far from the hiring finish line. The purpose of this interview is to **inspect what we're expecting.** We make assumptions and expectations based on what we've learned about this person up to this point. *Based on _____, I believe this person might _____,* and so on. This is where we get to see if our assumptions are correct or if we are surprised to learn something very different.

You may remember there were six applicants who caught my eye at Career Night. After the essay answers came back, I was once again left with about six applicants. Sometimes, you'll find those people stay the same, and sometimes, your mind is changed after you read through the essays. Regardless, you'll be left with a small group of (hopefully) strong candidates to choose from, filtered down more and more at each step of the process.

We stress **alignment** in this interview. Is this person aligned with our culture? Is this person aligned with the role they're applying for? We are searching for the motivation behind this person applying for this position at this time with this company. We want to get a general vibe of whether or not this person should continue in the process.

#6) **Conduct reference checks.**

Reference checks are a step that is often overlooked or misplaced in the process. It can be tempting to take people at face value, but we want to stress the importance of getting another perspective on this applicant from someone who knows them. Imagine you agree to marry someone but have never met their family or friends. You're trusting that person to be completely forthcoming about who they are without seeing the big picture and different vantage points that can lead to a much deeper understanding.

During these reference checks, it's important you commit to going **Three Deep.** Keller Williams has developed a Recruit-Select and Career Visioning Process that instructs leaders to select three references, ask them a series of questions, then ask each of those references to give you the name and information of one more person. Those initial references are very likely someone like an aunt, a best friend, and a boss they love. Of course, they won't say anything bad about the candidate. They're biased because they're loyal to the candidate. But the three names you're given next are people who may not have that same loyalty and proximity. You'll likely receive more honest answers because they haven't been tee-ed up as cheerleaders. The ideal end goal is to get yet another series of names from that bunch, but understandably, that is no easy feat. If you can get Three Deep with even one of the references, consider it a win.

#7) **Conduct a 3-hour interview.**

The Gilligan's Island crew was supposed to go on a three-hour tour, and it wound up being much longer than that. Well, a three-hour interview sure can feel a lot longer than three hours, but we have found it to be a gamechanger. We don't want anyone to feel married to the idea of a rigid time frame as each organization is going to have unique processes and needs, but that three-hour goal has worked well in our world. We break up the interview into a 90-minute deep dive into who they are, a 15–20-minute break, and a final 70-75 minutes of questions and answers. It's important you have a trusted team member in on this interview as well because differing perspectives can be crucial in the decision-making process. If you don't have a team, bring in someone from your brokerage, a spouse, or a friend to help you in this step.

The initial deep dive focuses on learning their story. *Who is this person?* The candidate is asked a series of questions that reveal truths about who they are, what they have gone through, and what has shaped them. *What were their highest highs? What moments nearly broke them?* This is not a time to be meek or shy. We value authenticity and vulnerability in this interview because we know that to share in this way takes a great deal of courage. The goal of the interviewer is to get the person off-script. When asked a question about their childhood, a candidate is likely to start giving a response they've recited before. That's not the answer you want. You want the answer below that one. If someone is willing to share that deeper answer, to walk through and retell stories of the messes they created or the hard lessons they learned through their mistakes, it doesn't look like brokenness. It looks like strength.

Through listening to their life story, you will begin to notice themes. *Is this person a victor or a victim? How do they recount the things that have happened in their life? How do they speak about other people?* Anyone in your ecosystem also needs to be coachable, so it's vital to be listening for that in their life story too. *Who influenced them? What motivated them?* You should also be assessing, *do you like this person?* Look for subtle body language, tone, and general attitude. *Do you trust them? Are they being authentic?* This person will be representing your brand out in the community, so your instincts are extremely important in this step.

Next is the 15–20-minute break. At this time, the candidate is asked to step out, and you are honest with them that you're going to talk a little behind their back. They can use that time to refill their coffee or water, use the restroom, and go for a quick walk around. But you use part of that time to check in with your co-interviewer. *What are our initial impressions? What are we thinking about this person? Any concerns we noticed?*

The first part of the interview focuses on connection, hunger, and values. That's what matters most. The specifics of the job don't even come into play until the second portion of this three-hour interview. This is when you will get into their qualifications, attitudes, energies, and strengths. That will help paint a clearer picture of whether or not they are a fit for the specific role they applied for. But we strongly believe in the power of unconventional methods to get remarkable results.

This second portion is also about asking hard questions. Sometimes, you will have concerns about a candidate, and you will need to ask some clarifying questions to validate that those assumptions are correct. If that's the case, there is no need to go the full 70+ minutes. You owe it to the candidate as well as yourself and your partner in that process to not waste time on something you know isn't going to be worth the investment. You can say something like, "I appreciate you applying. I wish this was the right fit, but my gut is just telling me it's not right now. Thanks for coming in." There's no reason to go through the motions and extend the interview any longer than it needs to be. Sometimes, people will get their feelings hurt by that kind of transparency and directness, but it's better to be honest than to be stuck with someone on your team who isn't the right fit.

#8) **Look for validation.**

You should never be the only person making this decision. This validation step is when you invite the department to go out of the office with this person, maybe to happy hour, lunch, or coffee. You want to make sure it's a social situation where you are able to see this person let their hair down. Those that come with you are not validating whether this person has the chops for the position. They're looking for whether or not they trust this person and if they enjoy spending time with them. Would they be proud to call this person a team member?

Another way to go about this step is to invite the candidate to dinner with their spouse or partner. This is not as crucial in an admin role, but in any sales or ISA position, the partner needs to be aware it is a lifestyle. The partner needs to be aware of the commitment involved. We had an ISA join the team years ago who was a rockstar right off the bat. He had a tech background, so he was able to come in and build us computers we are still using today. He absolutely crushed the role. But the first night he was on leads, he was out on a date with his wife. It's his responsibility as an ISA to respond to leads as they came in. Their date was interrupted twice because he had to connect with leads. This didn't go over well with his wife, and they quickly realized the familial sacrifices involved with this new, production-based role. Ultimately, he left Hatch for a more predictable 9-to-5.

Not everyone is going to be cut out for ISA or sales positions. The nights and weekends are not going to be a fit for every person. It's vital to be transparent with not only the candidate but also their spouse or partner so they can work together to make the decision that is best for them and their lifestyle.

#9) **Offer them the job.**

At long last, it's time to offer the best candidate the job. This should be done either face-to-face, voice-to-voice, or Zoom-to-Zoom. Now would be the time to show this person the energy and enthusiasm you have about their joining the team. Through the first eight steps of this lengthy process, that person has been held at arm's length. It's crucial they get to know at this point how excited you would be to have them on your team. Now is the time you would share things like benefits, compensation package, expectation of hours, and the licensing process, if needed. You also provide a paper copy of everything you share. When finished, you should email them a breakdown of all of the details. Once you offer the job, it's important you set a clear deadline of when you would like to hear back from them.

When offering a position to someone who still needs to get their real estate license, it is of the utmost importance to clearly communicate that the position is contingent upon them getting their real estate license. Wait to have them start the job until they have a license in hand. We have learned the hard way not to start the onboarding process with someone until they have shown commitment to the position by swiftly completing the steps necessary to obtain their real estate license.

We understand this hiring process is arduous, lengthy, and a huge investment of time and mental energy. We do not take that lightly, but we have seen firsthand the benefit of slowing down and hiring with care and intention. If you want to hire the right people, you can't do it quickly. Slow down enough to really get clear on if this is a person you enjoy spending time around, if they are a person you like and trust, and if you would feel comfortable with them representing you and your organization. To assist in this process, we have made our materials available for purchase. By going to **https://www.hatchcoaching.com/product/hire-like-hatch/** and purchasing our *Hire Like Hatch* online course, you can obtain full access to course videos as well as the ability to download our Reference Check Script, Phone Interview Template, Marco Polo Instructions, and Essay Questions.

TRAIN

Training, in its simplest form, is a process of **Watch Me, Watch You, then Go Do**. *Watch Me* provides the opportunity for someone to be in a leader's shadow. They observe, take notes, learn the basics, and get a general vibe for how things are done. *Watch You* is when the new team member is allowed to take on a more autonomous role but is given the benefit of real-time feedback and a sounding board for any concerns, questions, or frustrations. A common mistake many leaders make is skipping the *Watch You* stage and trusting people are ready to go out and do. Training is not something that can be a one-and-done process. It evolves over time, but it never stops. Training is learning, and we believe training happens for as long as someone is with the company. We do not train to standard; we train to excellence.

Hire on culture-train on skill.

*"You don't hire for skills-you hire for attitude.
You can always teach skills."*
- Simon Sinek

We have online training and onboarding courses available through Hatch Coaching that automate this process. Course One focuses on self-growth - encouraging and empowering individuals to get the right mindset and habits to excel both professionally as well as personally. Course Two is all about the lead-generation lifestyle - breaking down the idea that pouring into your community can also improve your business. Course Three is about the importance of role play - practicing and improving the way we live in community and serve people. And lastly, in Course Four, we finally address the nuts and bolts of this industry by talking about the paperwork and process items. But as you'll see in any of our materials, the emphasis is very little on real estate and heavily focused on people, communication, and the so-called *soft skills*.

Soft skills are really hard for a lot of people. Even those with strong interpersonal skills can be strengthened by solid mentorship and opportunity for feedback. It's important for team members to be poured into by their leaders on an intentional, scheduled, and daily basis in various ways. During the *Watch You* portion of training, it's imperative for a leader to give specific feedback in the moment to help someone get better. This is not a time to teach but a time to coach. Training needs to be customized and unique to that person. Their specific strengths and weaknesses are taken into consideration, and a game plan is created for them to improve. Anything less than that specialized degree of training will lead to mediocrity. We don't do mediocrity.

The Perfect (and Recommended) Daily Schedule

8:30 a.m. - train & role play
9:15 a.m. - lead generate
10:45 a.m. - quick meeting and prep for the day
11:00 a.m. - your day begins
   showings, lead follow up, inspections,
   consults, negotiations, etc.

Our perfect (and recommended) schedule to encourage this intentional growth starts with training and role playing right off the bat at 8:30. An hour and a half of lead generation follows at 9:15. A quick huddle begins at 10:45 for recapping victories, discussing what people are working on, checking score cards, and holding people accountable. From 11 a.m. on, the rest of the to-do lists begins - showings, lead follow up, inspection, consults, and negotiations.

RETAIN

There are two key elements of retention – **culture** and **proximity**. First, you need to create a culture worth sticking around for. Truthfully, *culture* is a watered-down word at this point. When we speak about culture, we need to see past the buzzwordiness of it and see it as more than ping-pong tables and potlucks, though there's nothing wrong with either. Culture is the feeling that everyone is playing, not only for themselves but also for the person next to them. Iron sharpens iron. Competition can exist in that culture, but that competition works to benefit the group as a whole. Culture means we are in this together.

The second element is *proximity*. You need to keep tending to your big pumpkins. Mike Michalowitz writes in *The Pumpkin Plan* about how to grow world-class, blue-ribbon winning pumpkins. Paralleling in leadership, we find leadership needs to plant the right seeds, weed out the losers, and nurture the winners - just like prize-winning pumpkin growers. He stresses the importance of spending the majority of your time with your big pumpkins. The most dangerous thing in any business is when those big pumpkins, those key players in your business, feel invisible or overlooked. A couple of years ago, one of our most beloved agents left our team to venture off on her own. It left a big crack in our foundation when she did. Her close friend, another strong agent, left shortly thereafter. I was completely taken by surprise, and I really don't like surprises.

Here's the deal – I wasn't tending my big pumpkins. I wasn't providing the tending and nurturing to those agents that they required to keep growing, and I learned from that experience. My team now knows they can come to me with any challenges or questions, if something doesn't feel right, or if they're running out of runway or opportunity. I can help find solutions for them to stay. If someone wants to make 100% on their transactions, I will never say "no." I will say, "Yes, when…" It is my duty and responsibility as the leader of this team to show them a path.

Leadership is a large part of retention, and what it ultimately boils down to is how connected people feel and to what degree they feel the organization is built with them in mind, not just the leader. A common misunderstanding is best splits will yield the most-satisfied employees, but that's not what we've observed. People certainly want to be appropriately compensated, but in order to be truly satisfied in their work, people need to feel seen or valued.

In order to attract and retain quality people, you either pay them the most or have the best opportunities to grow. Paying the most is a losing game. Someone will always come along and undercut you. You need to pay them the most you can, for sure, but more importantly, you need to provide them the best opportunity to grow.

Yes, When

- When a team member asks for something (a higher split, a chance to work with listings, they want the corner office, they want to work 10 hours/week, etc.), always meet them with "YES." Saying "no" tells them they don't have room to grow or customize their journey with you.

In 2020, I shifted from spending the majority of my time with our new people to investing most of it in our seasoned people. **Just because they have reached a point of competency**

or even excellence doesn't mean they're done growing. It's my responsibility to keep leading them, no matter how great they have become. That simple shift has almost completely eliminated the headaches I was experiencing before.

The Rule of 6:1

A leader should have no more than six people reporting to them/within their care at any given time.

Jesus had 12, and y'all ain't Jesus.

To accomplish this, every department needs to feel like a close team within the team. Each and every member of the business needs to have proximity to leadership to feel connected, seen, and valued. We have something called the Rule of 6:1 that says no one leader should have more than six people reporting to them.

Proximity & Customization

- Why will great talent stick around?
  - Because they have PROXIMITY to the leader.

- John Maxwell says he loves everybody on his team, but they have to earn his time. So the more someone develops, the more time they get with you.

- And because they have a CUSTOMIZED journey, you don't put them in a box. You develop a plan for them to reach their goals.

- *"If you hold somebody accountable to your goals, they'll resent you. If you hold them accountable to their goals, they'll thank you."* - Steve Kout

Chapter 3

Know Your Numbers

Numbers aren't necessarily sexy, but they're crucial to the overall health and viability of your business. Because we are talking about numbers throughout this chapter, you will notice it reads differently than the others. But in order to create a company that can withstand the various trials and tribulations that are inevitable over time, you need to get very clear on your numbers and financial footing, so it's important we make time to zoom in on these concepts.

3 Ways to Make More Money

There are three ways you can make more money – sell more, spend less, and find efficiencies. When you sell more, your Cost of Goods Sold (COGS) actually stays the same on a percentage basis. When you spend less, you lower your expenses that go out on a regular basis. When you find efficiencies, you maximize the opportunities you have by increasing your conversion rates and charging more. Examples of efficiencies could be things like increasing commissions or charging a transaction fee.

 **HATCH HINT**

3 Ways to Make More Money

1. **Sell more**
   More sales should lead to more profit.
2. **Spend less**
   Cutting unnecessary expenses and holding your money accountable can lead to extra cash.
3. **Find efficiencies**
   Charge a higher commission, increase conversion rates, charge a transaction fee, add vendor dollars, etc. All of these steps will lead to more money for you and the company.

3 Ways to Get Paid

As a business owner, you will need to pay yourself in three ways.

1. **Salary**: It's important you get paid a salary for the role you play. You need to get used to paying yourself monthly as an employee of your own company.

2. **Commission**: You should be paying yourself the same commission you would be paying any other agent on your team - not more, not less. This cash comes out of your business account and goes into your personal account every time commissions are paid. Commissions from your own personal production are to be included in *Cost of Goods Sold (COGS)*. Too many businesses have falsified numbers of what their financial health actually looks like because they are funding their business through their own personal production. In reality, they are paying to have a team. That will never be sustainable.

3. **As a Business Owner**: Yes, you get a salary, you get a commission, **and** you get paid as the owner of the business. We recommend 25%.

3 Ways to Get Paid

1. Salary
Pay yourself for working on the business.
If you were to replace yourself as CEO, what would that salary be?
2. Commission
Pay yourself the same commission other team members would make for their production.
This pay comes out of the company bucket and goes directly to you.
3. Owner Profit
This is what is left over after you pay all of your bills and commissions.

Ask yourself:

What am I getting paid as a producer?

What am I getting paid as an employee of the company?

What am I getting paid as a business owner?

When it comes time to file taxes, you will have been paid from all three of these accounts (COGS - your commission, Expenses - your salary, and Profit - your ownership privilege).

5 Numbers to Know in Order to Succeed

Our friend Andy Mulholland at Simple-Numbers.com does a great job of breaking down the 5 simple numbers we should know:

1. **Gross Commission Income** – This number is the total sum of all of the money, entire real estate commission check, and any transaction fees. This is **every single dollar** in.

2. **Cost of Goods Sold** – This is the sum of any commission you pay to your brokerage plus all of the commissions you are paying to the sales agents on your team as well as the commissions you are paying yourself, if you are an agent on your team.

3. **Gross Profit (Margin)** – This is the cost of goods sold subtracted from gross commission income.

4. **Expenses** – This number is the total cost of three expense categories - 1) People, 2) Marketing, and 3) Overhead.

5. **Net Profit** – This number is obtained by subtracting expenses from the gross margin.

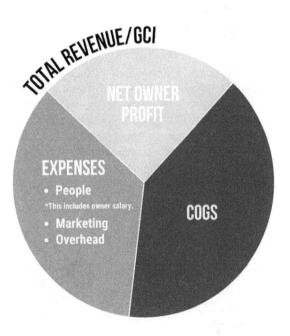

Do not lose sight of the fact that you are, in fact, getting paid three different ways as a business man/woman as you run your real estate team. You'll earn a salary as an employee, commission as a salesperson, and profit as a business owner. Your tax return will show all the cash you're making, and you need to track that also. If we begin with the end in mind, you'll need to ensure you're building on the right financial foundation from the beginning. If you don't have a healthy P&L, you won't have a healthy business.

Calculating Return on Investment

For calculating Return on Investment (ROI), let's imagine you're spending $1k a month on a lead source. You've put in $12k over one year on that lead source, and you've closed four deals through it. Your average commission on those deals is $8k. The four deals x $8k average commission brings you to $32k. Simply put, we should divide $32k by $12k, and you will discover you are getting a 2.67 ROI. But you have to remember you're paying your agents in production a 40% commission split, and 40% of $32k comes out to $12.800. You need to subtract that $12,800 from $32k which brings you down to $19,200. You recalculate ROI now using that updated number and discover the true ROI would be 1.6 ROI.

Our recommendation is you should aim to have a 3:1 minimal return on your investment. It must be noted, however, that long-term nurture leads take more time. It is hard to measure nurtures in the first six months. Things that are building reputation and mindshare are hard to quantify, but after 3-6 months, you should be starting to get a good idea of your ROI on low-hanging fruit.

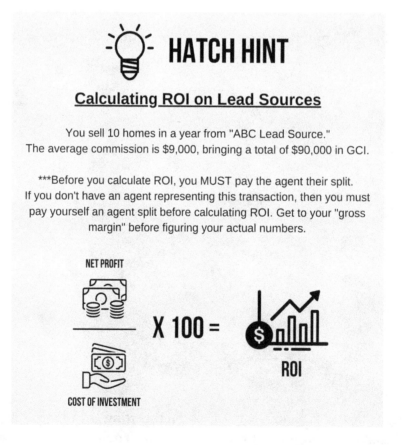

Rule of 20 to 1

As we've studied top real estate teams, there is a historic average of doing 20 transactions for every one team member. When factoring a team member's impact, it would be impossible to estimate correctly if all calculations began at day one. Admin starts day one, an ISA starts after six months, a new agent starts after six months, and a showing partner starts at day one. To calculate how many people you have on your team and you have an ISA who started last month, you don't count them. It's a "sunk cost" – you get nothing for it as a team.

Most teams that go "wide" with their approach see a much less attractive ratio of success. Teams that boast big sales but their ratio of sales to people looks something like 5:1 or 8:1 are not creating big lives for those agents. It's a revolving door for people who have the talented leave and so many others that don't make it. That's not a model that creates a winning culture.

20:1 is hard to achieve yet should be the North Star for many teams. It'll take massive focus and energy, yet it leads to the most unbelievable environment for all.

The Rule of 20:1

Erik surveyed some of the top teams in the country to find out their ratio of transactions to total team members (agents, admin, ISAs).

The Result?

A healthy team (with an average price point of 200k-350k) averaged 20 transactions for every one team member per year. It didn't matter if it was an agent, an admin, or an ISA. Adding one team member helped teams add 20 transactions to their team total annually on average.

*Healthy teams with an average sales price over 350k saw that number drop to something like 16:1.

**Healthy teams with an average sales price under 200k saw that number jump to something like 24:1.

***Adding a new agent (not a partner) to your ecosystem has a six-month ramp-up, so it is not recommended to count them in your ratio until the 7th month.

Red Light, Yellow Light, Green Light

It is imperative to get full clarity on the numbers and a comprehensive understanding of your financial reality so you have the confidence to spend more on growth and maintenance of your business when it is the right time to do so. We have witnessed people be incredibly irresponsible with their finances and wind up digging a hole they can't get out of when they haven't had a good grasp on the numbers. "When this next deal closes, then…" is a dangerous path to walk.

SAMPLE P & L

COGS	40%
Expenses	35%
Profit	25%

Expenses

OVERHEAD

Auto, auto insurance, gas	0.50%
Education and Coaching	3.00%
Dues & Subscriptions	0.25%
Insurance	0.50%
Entertainment and Meals	1.25%
Office Supplies, Professional fees, & Technology	2.00%
Listing Expenses	1.00%
Occupancy/Rent	2.50%
Travel	1.00%
Total Overhead:	**12%**

LEAD GENERATION

Lead Generation	9.00%

SALARIES/ BENEFITS

Salaries & Benefits	14.00%

If you follow the sample Profit and Loss (P&L) numbers above, you will keep yourself conservatively within the limits of what is tried and true for sustainable growth. Consider the following before deciding to grow:

- **Green Light:** Profit Numbers of 22.5% and Above

  This is the go zone. It is safe to assume you're in a financially stable enough position to grow. Feel free to take some financial risks when operating with a green light.

- **Yellow Light:** Profit Numbers of 17.5-22.5%

  In this range, it's wise to seek the guidance of a coach to help you through this decision because growth would mean you are skating on thin ice. It's not impossible, but it's risky. You'll want that second opinion to make an informed and thoughtful decision. Proceed with caution.

- **Red Light:** Below 17.5%

  This is the danger zone. You never want to spend your way out of troubles, and doing so in this range would put you in an awfully tight financial position. There should be no new expenses added until you get above the red light.

Of course, not every business is going to choose to follow our sample P&L numbers. We trust and recommend them, but ultimately, it is up to each business to do what works best for them. It is, however, absolutely necessary for a business to have a clearly defined red-light, yellow-light, and green-light ranges so they make logical and not emotional decisions.

Big 6 of Converting Business:

The Big 6 Conversion Metrics refer to the key numbers that tell the story of what you are doing to convert your leads. These six metrics are:

1. Lead to Appointment Set
2. Appointment Set to Appointment Met
3. Appointment Met to Committed
4. Committed to Writing an Offer
5. Offer to Pending
6. Pending to Close

Your understanding of these numbers is going to radically improve the strength of your entire ship. These numbers and the tracking of them is imperative to have long-term success in this business. We have already discussed there are three ways to make more money: you spend less, you earn more, and you find efficiency. The game is really won when you can find the efficiencies. By honing in and understanding these conversion metrics, you don't have to go out and buy more business. You just need to be better with the business you have.

Years ago, I was connected to a Facebook group, and people in the group were talking about their show rates, the rate at which people show up to the appointments set by an ISA. One person who was known for having a strong ISA department, someone who was teaching and coaching others how to do it, reported a show rate of 50%. I remember being so surprised that I went to Robby T., our ISA lead at the time, and asked if that could possibly be true. Hatch Realty had a show rate of over 80% - far exceeding some of the best in the game, and I recognized we had really cracked the code on something really special.

Far too many people focus on buying leads when what they should really be focusing on is protecting their marketing dollars. Each team is going to differ when it comes to pain points in lead conversion. These metrics help narrow in and identify where those pain points are happening. For example, if your Set-to-Met ratio is 20% - far below our recommended number you will see below - then that can help you identify it as a pain point. These metrics help pinpoint the leading indicators of where you will need to focus your energy and attention in the lead conversion game. For example, if your Met-to-Committed ratio is low, you then know you need to work with your agents to help them understand how they need to earn people's business. You can really start pulling on the levers and figuring out the best strategy for your business, filling in any of the gaps you find.

The Big 6 Conversion Metrics

Lead To Appointment Set
5-7% *depends on lead source*

Set To Met Ratio
Buy Side   Sell Side
65%   90%

Met To Committed Ratio
Buy Side   Sell Side
90%   65%

Committed to Offer Ratio
Buy Side   Sell Side
50%   95%

Offer to Pending Ratio
Buy Side Sell Side
MARKET SPECIFIC

Pending To Close
Buy Side   Sell Side
95%   95%

Total Set to Close Ratio
Buy Side   Sell Side
27.78%   52.79%

Chapter 4
How to Lead Yourself

It seems serendipitous that I, Robby Trefethren (better known to those in the real estate world as the lead geek "Robby T."), take over on the How to Lead Yourself section because that's exactly what I had to do to get where I'm at now. Here's the cliff-notes version of my story. I was born and raised in Fargo, North Dakota, in a working-class household. I was a pathetic high school student who skipped as many classes as I attended. I barely graduated on time and was told by my high school counselor that he didn't think I was cut out for a four-year university. I took a gap year in an attempt to figure out what I wanted, met the lovely woman who is now my wife, fell in love with reading and bettering myself, and managed to get accepted into a transitional, probationary program at a local university. I was hellbent on proving my high school counselor wrong.

I worked full-time jobs throughout college to pay my way since my family wasn't able to help me financially at the time, and I minimized my debt as much as possible. I quickly learned the importance of time management and prioritizing the important shit. I graduated Summa Cum Laude while working a full-time political job and trying to build a good life for myself and my new wife. We found out we were expecting our first child rather unexpectedly in the summer of 2013. We definitely wanted a family *someday,* but we didn't feel ready when that someday turned into *nine months from now.* My wife had just started grad school and had quit her barista job to focus on school. I had been let go from a political campaign that I was too green and immature to be leading.

We were a couple of unemployed 23-year-olds with a baby on the way. We were terrified. Up to that point, I had been driven by a desire to prove people wrong, but I felt something change within me as we anxiously anticipated the birth of our firstborn child. I wanted to **prove myself right.** I knew I had it in me to build a big life. I knew I was capable of not only providing for my family but thriving with my family. I knew that even though times were tough, we would figure it out.

I had worked on Josh Boschee's political campaign in the fall of 2012 as he ran for a state office. Josh was also the original ISA at Hatch Realty. We ran into each other at a political event late in 2013, and he let me know about an opening at Hatch Realty. They were looking to expand their ISA department, and he thought I could be perfect for it. He encouraged me to apply, but I originally laughed it off, insisting I had no interest in real estate.

After more thought and several more weeks of watching our bank account drain, I decided to reach back out to Josh and apply for the job. I managed to land an interview and showed up in an ill-fitting suit. I dropped a couple of F-bombs in the process, but by the grace of God, they still gave me a shot. Josh's strong bid of confidence was the nudge Erik needed to offer me the position. I'm so grateful every single day that they took a chance on me.

I started as an ISA and worked in that role for 2.5 years. Throughout that time, I made over 100,000 phone calls, spoke to more than 10,000 people, and set over 1,000 appointments which led to over 450 closings. There were almost no other ISAs seeing anywhere near that kind of success at the time. Naturally, people were growing curious about how to replicate that kind of success in their own businesses.

Fast forward to five years later, I'm now nationally recognized as the voice of authority within the ISA and lead conversion game. We have two areas of expertise at Hatch Coaching – redefining how people treat clients and redefining how people treat their team members. My day-to-day work includes massive amounts of pouring into others in order for their clients and team to feel seen, heard, and valued. But in order to do that work, in order to truly show up for my own clients and my own family, it's crucial that I first and foremost follow a diligent regimen of self-leadership.

Throughout my time in business, one thing has become increasingly clear – the quality of your business will be directly tied to the amount of personal investment you do. Warren Buffet, the greatest investor of all time, says the most lucrative investment you can ever make is not a specific stock or business model but the gift of time and investment in yourself.

When we think about where people fall on a spectrum of self-investment, I like to categorize certain mindsets and behaviors into what I call the 4 Growth Zones:

1. **Regression Zone** – People in this zone may have some great ideas or skills, but they fail to do anything with them. Just like a muscle, those skills start to deteriorate over time when they're not put into action.

2. **Comfort Zone** – We've all heard of this one. People in this zone may be putting things into action, but they are doing the same things over and over again. They're not pushing themselves to be better. They've plateaued. Using that same muscle analogy, consider this – the people may have a consistent workout routine, but they do the exact same resistance, reps, and angles every single time. They're not trying to grow; they're keeping the status quo.

3. **Growth Zone** – People in this zone consistently push themselves just beyond their comfort zone. They prioritize learning and implementing new ideas. In the gym, this would mean increasing resistance, increasing reps, and trying new things. In terms of personal investment, this means increasing resistance by listening to conflicting ideas, increasing time dedicated toward personal growth, and trying new things to become a more self-aware individual.

4. **No Growth Zone** – People in this zone are asking too much of themselves without setting appropriate goals or limits. They may be setting unrealistic goals then getting defeated when they don't achieve them. They may be taking on too many projects or responsibilities and spreading themselves too thin. They may not be resting appropriately or getting enough sleep. They're overextending and overexerting themselves, possibly doing more damage than good.

It's important to live as often as possible inside of your growth zone. Personal investment compounded daily is the only way to sustain growth. This can look like reading, studying, practicing, trying new things, exposing yourself to new ideas, being willing to unlearn what you've learned, and mastering new subjects consistently. It's vital to never stop learning. The medium to do those things may vary from person to person. For some people, the resources are books. For others, it's podcasts, YouTube videos, or webinars, but the main idea is to study ideas outside of your own. Studying means doing nothing else except focusing on the material being presented. Notes are essential. Working out and listening to a podcast isn't studying. That's high-quality entertainment.

In the world of real estate, there are natural ups and downs in the market and in the year. Very rarely is a realtor's year completely steady. When things slow down, it's an opportunity to increase the time invested in yourself. Many realtors will focus on the dip in the market and find reasons to complain. But successful people turn their disadvantages into their advantages. Let's take a global pandemic as an example. Fear ruled a lot of agents, but top producers were those who lead generated and invested in themselves despite the setback. They turned those setbacks into their opportunities. Top agents and teams will tell you market shifts and declines are actually your best opportunities to leapfrog your competition.

But self-investment isn't only mental; it's physical too. It's important to remember that how we treat our physical bodies has a direct link to our mental performance. Take a quick personal inventory – *How am I eating? How am I sleeping? Am I finding consistent, enjoyable ways to move my body?* Physical movement and exercise drastically increase the performance of your brain (Mandolesi, L. et al, 2013). Lack of physical movement correlates to lower brain performance. This also applies to what you eat. The food you eat, the sugar you consume, the amount of water you drink - it all affects the brain and the subsequent energy you have to perform throughout the day. We are better at making mental decisions when we treat our bodies right.

There seems to be an emphasis on hustle in our current business culture. Keep grinding, keep moving, and don't stop. Rest is not the opposite of discipline. Rest is **required** for discipline. Burnout is inevitable if you are not allowing yourself to slow down. It is estimated that a person makes about 35,000 decisions a day (Sahakian & Labuzetta, 2013). Sleep is how we refuel our brain, and it is vital to create a healthy sleep routine to maximize efficiency and mental clarity. Be disciplined in your work, for sure, but be disciplined in your rest and sleep too.

Motivational speaker Jim Rohn famously said that you become the average of the five people you spend the most time with. Find people you respect and admire, and carve out intentional time with them. Seek their guidance and advice when making a big decision. Ask for their feedback on blind spots you may see in terms of your personality or habits. Be brave enough to ask for help when you need it. Surround yourself with the kind of people you want to be like, and watch how your life changes.

Lastly, it's important to note that people will judge you for your self-investment. Your uncommon habits are likely going to be the subject of criticism from common people. You have to have the mental fortitude to focus on where you're wanting to go and not get hung up on the opinions of others. People may think you're weird for choosing the habits you do. Family may be disappointed in you or confused by your priorities if they do not value the same kind of self-investment. They may not understand the decisions you're making or the investment you're pouring into yourself, and you may even feel lonely on that journey at times. Let that be okay. Allow yourself to be uncomfortable with it. The most important investment you will ever make is to invest in yourself. Focus on that, and keep moving forward.

Throughout this book, you will see that Erik and I take turns leading certain sections. We appreciate your patience in that and will do our best to differentiate the changes as clearly as we can. I'm going to toss it back to Erik at this point to explain our next chapter on leading others, something the man has mastered over the last couple of decades.

Chapter 5

How to Lead Others

Leadership works best when it is proactive instead of reactive. That proactivity requires showing up for people in both the **scheduled** and the **sporadic**. Showing up in scheduled ways looks like one-on-ones, small-group meetings, and large-group meetings. But it's not enough just to show up. It's imperative to genuinely love running those meetings because, put simply, people can smell bullshit from a mile away. Go in with a topic and energy, but remember not to talk at people; you want to talk with people. The main goal is to get those in the room to self-discover. It's far better to hold them accountable to what they want than to do so with what you want for them. We recommend one-on-one weekly meetings for 60 minutes for the first six months, then 30 minutes every week or 45 minutes every two weeks after that.

In the 1980s and 90s, it was very possible to leave work at work. But times have changed, and our growing interconnectedness means societal norms are very different now. Technology and mounting pressures follow us everywhere. We need to lean into that instead of fighting it and allow it to give us a clearer picture of what people are going through. This may be the first time you're reading something like that, and it may be uncomfortable. People could argue the need for stronger work/life separation and not allowing too much interlap.

However, it's undeniable that tough life circumstances impact someone's work and vice versa. My first book, *Play For The Person Next To You*, has an entire chapter called "You Can't NOT Have Cancer at Work." We often see it as crossing boundaries to acknowledge what is real and true in someone's life. There are various circumstances that can drastically impact someone's work life capacity — divorce, disease, debt, and grief, just to name a few. Ignoring or minimizing those things is not what is best for the person, and it is not healthy for the business. When someone is going through hell, we as an organization can walk alongside them and give them a hand. People only bring their best when they feel their best, and people feel worse for longer if it goes undiscussed. We are in the business of seeing our team members as whole people with rich and complicated lives. We are here to support them in any way we can.

To gain that kind of clarity, we see huge value in establishing and understanding their why, goals, and commitments from the very start. In those first few one-on-ones, it's important for a leader to get clear on a couple of questions. *What is all of this for? What is motivating them to be successful?* This may take a few sessions. That's absolutely time well spent.

Once a leader has a sense of a team member's why and what motivates them to be successful, the one-on-one sessions from that point on can follow this general format:

1. **Personal** – Start by making a personal connection, asking about life at home. Address any difficulties that are going on, refer back to the issues they shared before, and remember to be specific. Remembering a specific challenge they shared previously will show you are truly listening and care about them.

2. **Triage** – What in their business is suffering today? Where are they stumbling? What roadblocks are preventing them from reaching their goal? This is where things can go sideways a bit. That's okay.

   Let's imagine you have a teammate who has a goal to swim to a lighthouse two miles from shore. Yeah, this is completely unrelated to real estate, but just go with it. If you know about their goal to swim to the lighthouse but notice they're taking on water, you need to go and help them through that moment first and help them catch their breath. You would never watch someone drown and continue yelling their goal at them. That's never going to help.

   That catch-your-breath moment may take the remainder of the meeting. Allow space for it. This is when you get brought into their pain and help them through it. You can eventually use that understanding to help propel them to reach their goals. Slow down. Take the time to meet them in that fear and uncertainty. It's worth it.

3. **Growth Progression** – How is this person progressing? Are they taking active strides toward their goals? Sure, you can tell them how they're doing, yet it's far better for them to evaluate themselves. There's power in self-discovery! Inspect what you expect. See where the opportunities lie. What needs more discipline? What books do they need? Do they need a break or a vacation? What do they need to hear in order to self-discover that? Move the needle forward and help them reach their goals!

4. **Homework Assignment** – What would help get this person even one small step closer to their goal? Sometimes, this means having a hard conversation with a teammate. Sometimes, it means taking a couple of days off. Sometimes, it means finding a new system to hold themselves accountable. This is going to be specific and tailored to the unique needs of each person and their goals.

Leadership means helping each team member clearly understand the difference between **standards, goals, and possibilities**. Every great organization needs **standards** that everyone is held to, but unfortunately, many don't have standards. They have mere *suggestions*. People don't need suggestions and neither does an organization because suggestions don't lead to profitability. People need *explicit* clarity on standards to thrive. In order for a suggestion to become a standard, a consequence needs to be married to it. The best method is not to assign standards to people but to allow people to create the standards with you. What do they want? Who do they want to be? What should happen if they fall short of that?

But there's something fundamental that is even more important than standards. Keith Cunningham explains in his book *The Road Less Stupid* that people who irritate us the most are not usually those who fall short of the standard. Sure, not showing up to work on time is annoying, or not responding to an email is inconsiderate. However, that is not what drives people nuts. It's the people violating the rules of **culture** who cause the most hurt within the organization. It's the person who comes in day after day with a bad attitude and doesn't necessarily get a consequence who can start to cause rotting morale within the company.

It's vital to allow the whole group to define the culture of the organization because it is what they value as a group and a work family that will become the backbone of the company. They create a list of values and boundaries of what is okay within the ecosystem as well as what is not. This clearly defines things and puts the power in the hands of the team. There is ownership in this and an accountability that cannot be created from the top down.

With a clearly defined culture and standards in place, it's possible for **goals** to be set. Goals are set above the standard. It's not uncommon but truly unfortunate that many times leaders aren't even aware of someone's goals or their why. But make no mistake. That's not leadership. That's management. Understanding someone's goals is going to be the fuel that helps propel them forward. It's only by getting clear on that person's why, their motivation, and their drive that you can help them discover their potential.

And in our world, that potential is what we call **possibility**. Leaders are responsible for pouring into their team by talking not only about what is and what we hope to become but about the vast landscape on the horizon, one that maybe nobody else can see quite yet. We are responsible for creating the vision of what we are capable of. Leaders need the confidence and enthusiasm to invigorate and inspire their teams to see that potential and possibility too.

We create a culture of high standards, goals, and possibilities in many ways.

1. **Lead Over Lag** – Instill in yourself and your team the idea that we value lead measures, not lag. Lead is an independent commitment. Lag is a dependent result. "I want to sell more houses" is lag. That's not what we focus on. Lead is all of the measures that will make it happen. Lead is what you can put your fingers on, and it's what matters. Something like the number of contacts you'll make daily, the hours you commit to lead generation, or the total conversations you have would be good examples of lead measures.

2. **Scorecards and Scoreboards** – Everyone needs to know their numbers and how they stack up and be able to use that to fuel competition. Everything needs to be measured, and people need to understand those measurements. They should know how they are doing in comparison to each other, so take the metrics and make them visible. It's important to have a manual tracking system where you physically enter the numbers, because digital tracking, over time, becomes invisible. People need to see the numbers consistently for them to be of any competitive value.

3. **Create a Culture of Accountability** – Small groups of accountability buddies can help normalize and streamline this. Regularly checking in with each other creates a sense of trust and shared success. Additionally, as a whole, it's important to normalize talking about the numbers. Discussing the metrics needs to be as normal in your culture as talking about lunch or weekend plans.

4. **Get Curious** – A-players, the people who show up and consistently set the culture you want, are a leader's dream. But what happens when someone is struggling? First, the leader has to ask themselves, "Does this person know they are being destructive/hurtful?" If not, then it is your job to go directly to them and assume positive intent. Come from curiosity and ask questions before making any statements. If they are not self-aware, your responsibility is to help them self-discover. We can do that through the use of great questions and I-feel statements. *Examples*: "I'm noticing you're not as responsive to emails as you have been previously, and I'm concerned about you. Are you doing okay?" or "I feel worried when you're not following through on your commitments. Tell me more about what you've been dealing with lately."

5. **Make a Plan** – If the questions are asked, the problem is presented, the support is provided, and that person is still unable to self-discover, then you need to clearly communicate the message and help them make a plan to make it better. If someone isn't meeting their metrics, either culturally or performance-wise, a PIP (performance improvement plan) is put in place. Historically, PIPs fail about 80% of the time, but we believe that reflects more on poor leadership than anything else. It is absolutely crucial that when someone is clearly struggling, a leader comes alongside and makes a recommitment to them. Telling someone they're falling short isn't going to make them better, but providing the support needed to catch their breath just may give them a shot.

Difficult conversations can be tricky for many of us. When we have critical feedback to give, it can be helpful to gauge what the recipient is ready to hear at that moment. In getting their buy-in, you have welcomed them in and allowed them to take a greater degree of ownership in the conversation.

A Great Question to Ask:

"On a scale of 1-10 with one being meek and 10 being brutally honest, how honest would you like me to be with you?"

Chapter 6
Where to Get Business

4 Different Types of Lead Opportunities

1. **PCSOI** - Friends, Family, Past Clients, Classmates, Former Co-workers, Friends of Friends, Extended Family, Members of Community, Social Groups, Networking Groups
2. **Low-Hanging Fruit** - Property Inquiry Leads, CMA Request Leads, Come List Me Leads, Come Buy Me Leads, Referral Lead Sources, Radio and Television Advertising, Zillow Leads, Realtor.com Leads, Google Local Services, Dave Ramsey Leads, Referral Exchange, Homelight, Etc.
3. **Nurtures** - Forced Registration Leads, Home Evaluation Leads, Buyer Pay-per-Click or Seller Pay Per Click (through Google, Bing, Yahoo, Etc.), Social Leads (through Facebook, Instagram, etc.)
4. **Reputation** - Reviews, Word of Mouth, Advertising, Come List Me Leads, Come Buy Me Leads, Radio and Television Advertising, Google Local Services

There are four different types of lead opportunities in this business: 1) PCSOI (past clients and sphere of influence), 2) Low-Hanging Fruit, 3) Nurtures, and 4) Reputation. Each source can be valuable, so it's important to maximize time, energy, and resources by having a strategy in mind for each.

The good news about PCSOI is that it's free! The bad news? It can take years of nurturing to really cash out on it. PCSOI is the most reliable, sustainable, and ideal lead source you can create. But there are a couple of consistent reasons why we lose in this realm. Sometimes, we get out-relationshipped. We may have just crushed it in a meeting with a client and are feeling confident about it, but then we get a call the next day saying they are going with their cousin instead. I've been there. The second way we lose out on PCSOI is when we slam our foot on the gas pedal and transactionalize this bucket instead of nurturing it. People hate feeling monetized and used in that way and naturally choose another realtor instead.

At the beginning of my career, my admin Kim referred me to one of her old co-workers from the National Guard. I went over to meet the man, walked around the house like I always do, sat down at the kitchen table, and immediately pulled out my iPad 2. If that doesn't date me, I'm not sure what does. I scrolled through 30+ slides, telling him how great I was and all of the value I was going to bring. He didn't sign right away which didn't strike me as odd. Plenty of people hold off a day or two before choosing to make things official. I assumed the business and headed back to the office.

When I got there, Kim was infuriated. I was baffled. *What could I have possibly done wrong? I killed it!* But Kim set the record straight. He **hated** me. She reported back to me all of the ways I had transactionalized her friend. I failed to make a connection with him. I didn't get curious about who he was or how to best meet his needs. I didn't ask questions. I didn't work to build rapport and relationship with this man. I assumed that because Kim already had the relationship, I had it too. I didn't. I let Kim down, and I let her friend down.

There's a big myth about building SOI that you should reach out and ask people for their business. That's not it, friends. When I look around at the people killing it with their SOI, they're not asking for business. **They're attracting business.** People are reaching out to them because of who they are and how they make them feel.

Mindshare is key in terms of attracting business. It is the idea people have of you and the reputation you have created. It refers to your visibility, popularity, or recognizability within a given population. Through my work in youth ministry, I had built mindshare in the Fargo area as a caretaker in the community. I had the trust of hundreds and maybe thousands of people before I sold a single house, but I needed to figure out how to translate that trust into business. It was bar none the hardest path to go down, but I also believe it is the most profitable.

Don't worry. I'm not saying you should become a youth minister to succeed in real estate, but you do need to figure out how to build your own brand and mindshare in your community. Robby T. built mindshare in the real estate world as a flat-bill wearing, fast-talking, curse word-dropping, lead geek with glasses and beard with sheer grit and tenacity. He hustled his way up the ladder through creating products and systems that made a name for themselves through word of mouth. He's trusted around the country because he creates quality products that yield reliable results.

In order to make the most out of your PCSOI, it's important to remember the best CRM is at the tips of your fingers anytime, anywhere. I bet it's on your phone right now. It's social media, specifically Facebook. Facebook is not without its cringe-inducing elements, from political rants to comment-thread name calling, but ultimately, it is also a community rich with opportunity. These are people who are already engaged in your life. They are choosing to follow you and stay updated on what you share. It doesn't cost you anything except time.

So social media use in your business needs to be thoughtful. Consider this question: am I networking, or am I NOT working? Try to stick to the 80/20 rule. 80% of your social media posts should be about you and your real life. Not open houses. Not new listings.

You. Your family, your trips, your hobbies, and your thoughts. The remaining 20% of the content should be reminding people of what you do without hard selling. Get creative. Utilize a few hashtags to increase visibility. Check-in at locations to remind people of where you work or where you are. More than anything, narratives will capture people's attention, so storytelling is the best tool in your belt.

A common misconception for those who consider themselves less than tech savvy or perhaps just "not good at social media" is they can't succeed in that space. Maybe you're not an engaging person online, but that doesn't mean you can't succeed on social media. You get the option to be the most ENGAGED on social media. Like your friend's posts. Comment on their photos. Share others' successes. Be visible through cheerleading for others.

Facebook reminds us of birthdays each day. On any given birthday, someone could expect maybe a hundred FB wall posts and a dozen messages or so. But we don't want to be in the hundreds or even within that dozen. We want to be remarkable. A card or a phone call is engaging and different. Being remarkable will cost time and maybe even some money, and there may be no clear way to assess ROI, but it is worth it.

In terms of posting, keep it simple. Here is a hack. Rip off and duplicate. Repost the same great content you did a year or two before. People forget, so work smarter, not harder. Remember social media time is research time. Take notice of what gets traction for you and what doesn't. Simple questions like, "What's your favorite food for Thanksgiving?" or "What's your least favorite Halloween candy?" can get a ton of engagement. Be consistent and authentic. People can smell crap from a mile away.

But the highest monetization of social media is using it as a tool to engage with people offline. Take this real-life example from a couple of years ago. Robby and his wife, Lauren, had just welcomed their third baby. The baby had come home briefly but had developed severe jaundice to a point of requiring multiple days of hospitalization. Lauren posted about her fear and anxiety, watching her newborn baby under the lights and not being able to hold her, and requesting prayers for quick healing. I could have liked, maybe commented, and sent some prayers for their baby girl and felt that was enough. It's a great start, but showing up at the hospital with a meal was what they really needed. They needed someone to step in and support them through an emotionally draining time. Acts like that should never be done with the intention of earning business, but by stepping up and offering a hand when people need it, you build trust. Any additional business earned would be a cherry on top.

Connection Spectrum

When it comes to real connection which ultimately builds trust and mindshare, there are various things you can attempt. We have created the Connection Spectrum to explain what we see least impactful to most impactful so you can spend more of your time doing the things that will reap the most reward.

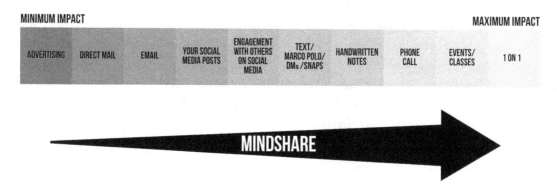

The first three strategies on the far left of the spectrum - advertising, direct mail, and email - provide very little impact in terms of connection. These items can be easily scaled and hired out, but they are also impersonal. They don't have much personality to them, and many potential clients see right through that as spam. These items alone aren't effective, but they can be part of a layering strategy.

The farther right you move along the spectrum, the more you are increasing connection and mindshare. These middle strategies - social media posts, engagement on social media, texts and messages, and handwritten notes - are not very scalable, but they are customized. They require you take intentional time to go deeper instead of wider. These middle spectrum items are important, but the maximum impact strategies go one step further.

On the far-right hand side of the spectrum, we have phone calls, events/classes, and 1-on-1 meetings. These strategies foster the greatest level of connection and, in turn, mindshare because they provide opportunity for honest rapport and relationship building to occur in real time. Voice-to-voice or face-to-face interactions remain the most effective because we are social creatures longing to be truly seen and understood. These types of interactions are not at all scalable, but they are worth every bit of effort you put into them because they are real, honest, and the most effective. The more energy and time you can spend on the far right of this Connection Spectrum, the better results you'll yield over time.

Client Events

Client events, when done well, can increase mindshare, and increased mindshare can increase market share. The true purpose of client events is to have your community feel seen, heard, valued, and cared for. These events are not only for clients but potential clients, friends, family members, and the community as a whole. It's not about the past but about potential.

There are two types of client events – **engage** events and **give** events. **Engage** events are niche and ask people to give their time. An example of this in our world would be Hatchstock, an annual event where we have rented bounce houses, local food vendors, and musical acts and throw a mini-festival in our parking lot. The other type are **give** events. These are quick and universal. Our Date Night event before Valentine's Day and our Pie Day event before Thanksgiving are examples of this. You give people free wine, beer, pizza, or pie, and your mindshare improves instantly. People love free.

But more than that, people like feeling you care about them. The beauty of events is not in the actual event but in the feeling you are giving to that person. The opportunity and the greatest win is in the follow up. Check in with the people who showed up to Pie Day and ask how their Thanksgiving went. Reach out for connection after the fact. We encourage the rule of Invite, Invite, Thank.

First Invite: "Hey Jason, I saw that Colin had an awesome hockey game last weekend. He's getting so big. I haven't seen you guys in so long! Come on by this week and get a pie at Hatch Pie Day." Note that you may have to reach out 3-5x in order to actually elicit a response.

Second Invite: "Just a reminder that Hatch Pie Day is tomorrow, so don't forget to pick up your pie. I'll be there all evening, so I'll be keeping an eye out. Hope to see you then!"

Thank: "It was really great seeing you last week at Hatch Pie Day. I hope you and the family had a great Thanksgiving. Tell Mary hi for me!"

That initial text or call shouldn't be focused on business, but at the end of that conversation, ask something like, "Can I give you a call next week for a quick business conversation?" There is a small window after numerous contact points in which you have earned the right for a business conversation. It is imperative that you do not blur the give with the business discussions. Instead, ask for an additional call later.

One big mistake many people make is they have big events and spam people by hard selling and asking for too much without a real connection. It comes off to the client or potential client as sales-y and off putting - the exact opposite of what should be happening. Instead, it is important you make these events into an opportunity to intentionally nurture connections.

We have to teach our people how to give us referrals. This is the purpose of your "business" call. It can be awkward and uncomfortable, but it's needed to grow. Share with your friend, "I'm really wanting to grow my referral business next year, and if you think I'm worthy of a referral, here's how you can help me out…" Encourage that friend to start a conversation, sort of handing them off via text or social media message. Communication and assertiveness skills do not come naturally to everyone, and it is only through explicit instruction that we can expect people to learn and grow.

Systems

Automation is the enemy of PCSOI. Our past clients and those individuals in our sphere of influence are the most likely to contact us with future business. It's estimated that two out of every 20 people we know should be giving us business each year. One of the 20 should be a referral and the other one of the 20 should come from direct business from that relationship. They are our people, and they deserve special, customized attention. We recommend 12 check-ins or touches each year. Here is how we make that happen at Hatch.

Each agent invites their PCSOI to our two Hatch Events (Date Night and Pie Day) every year. Three touches happen for each of those events: one invite, one reminder, and one thank you. Those invites, reminders, and thanks yous alone put them at six touches. The other six touches happen throughout the year, scheduled out in CRM reminders. These can be phone calls, social media messages, birthdays, house-versaries, or a variety of things.

Low-Hanging Fruit and Nurtures

Low-hanging fruit refers to the most expensive leads which are also the most likely to convert. Property Inquiry Leads such as Zillow, Realtor.com, Veterans United, and Homelight tend to convert quickly, usually within a few months. Nurture leads are pay-per-click or social media leads that are forced registration. These leads generally require long-term nurturing to convert at high levels, even up to a year or more. The game you play with both low-hanging fruit and long-term nurtures are the same.

Creativity is key in getting the team fired up about lead conversion. At Hatch, we have adopted the habit of including a Realtor Workout of the Day (RWOD) to transform the monotonous into something amusing and exciting.

REALTOR WORKOUT OF THE DAY

Examples:

Tuesday the 11th - 20-Contact Tuesday. Lead follow up with your Bs, Cs, and Ds.

Wednesday the 12th - Find at least three CURRENT CLIENTS to write a Zillow review.

Thursday the 13th - Hand-Cramp Thursday. Write 13 cards on the 13th! Doesn't matter to who.

Friday the 14th - Make at least 10 connections with people just to tell them how much you love and appreciate them.

Monday the 17th - Business-Card Monday. Connect with at least 10 people to give them your business card. You must COLLECT at least 20 cards as well.

Tuesday the 18th - Texting Tuesday. Send at least 30 text messages to people with a message that reads something like this, "Hey, I've been thinking about you lately. Is there anything I can do to help you as a friend/client/family member?"

Wednesday the 19th - Random-Acts-of-Kindness Day (RAK). Do something kind for at least two people. Tip HUGE. Pay for someone's coffee. Help a stranger or someone who needs an extra hand just because it's the right thing to do.

Thursday the 20th - Dumpster dive for people we've never been able to get in contact with. Every cleaned dumpster-dive client results in a $100 bonus at closing for you. Call, text, email. REPEAT.

Friday the 21st - Farming Friday. Knock on at least 30 doors to offer home valuations.

www.hatchcoaching.com

REALTOR WORKOUT OF THE DAY

How to set up a great RWOD:

1. Have a specific time each day that you and your team members will be doing this lead gen activity. Have it scheduled.

2. Don't assume they know what to say and what to do. ROLE PLAY and practice before you do this!

3. When you're done, gather again to establish what you learned - what worked/what didn't - and what success people had.

4. A great RWOD has 3 elements: Who, What, & How many (IE "Expired sellers" + "phone call" + 10 contacts)

5. To prepare, make a list of at least 20 "WHOs" and a list of at least 15 "WHATs" - this allows you to interchange and build a really robust RWOD plan.

6. Deep is better than wide. You may need to stay on the same WHO for more than a few days to work toward mastery.

Example of WHOs
Open house clients
As, Bs, Cs, or Ds
Past clients
Have not mets
Sphere
Vendors
Social media connections
Your wedding list/Christmas card list
Leads from _____ lead source (lots of options here)
Neighbors
SO MANY MORE (please work on adding at least 10 more WHOs to this list)

www.hatchcoaching.com

3 Core Principles of Lead Conversion:

These three principles are key in lead conversion. If you're wanting to surpass expectations and be extraordinary in the lead conversion game, these principles should be adopted by the team.

1) **Speed to Lead**

   This refers to how quickly you get to a lead. You need to be reaching out as quickly as possible. Ideally, this is done within minutes via text, call, or email.

   - *Nurture Leads* – We at Hatch Coaching are often asked whether phone calls or texts are more effective. Truthfully, it depends entirely on your market. Calling isn't worth the effort in a young market but would be more effective with older clients. We would recommend split testing whether or not phone calls make sense for you.

- *Low-Hanging Fruit* – Call no matter what.

2) Speed to Response

If someone texts you back, speed to response refers to how quickly you are texting back again. Imagine how it would feel to be left hanging when you are trying to connect with someone. If you leave someone on read with no response, that's not a good look!

3) Speed to Value

This refers to how well you engage in a conversation to help them get what they want as soon as possible. If someone wants to go see a home and you don't make it happen for three days, that's not going to sit well with an excited homebuyer.

Reputation

Reputation is the germination of mindshare and investment into your branding. Radio, billboards, referrals, and reviews can all serve as bricks with the ability to build a strong foundational reputation in your community. But not all bricks are the same. Earned reputation is where you need to invest your time and energy. PCSOI and reviews are earned, and they are incredibly valuable. We live in a review culture - Google, Facebook, Yelp, Zillow, and more. The most important place for reviews is ever-changing. A few years ago, Zillow reviews were everything. Now, Google reviews seem like the gold standard. By the time you're reading this, it could be something else entirely. Reviews are an imperative piece of reputation, and it's important to know where the eyeballs are. Be willing to pivot as trends change.

Paid reputation, on the other hand, is not always worth the time or money, so it's important to be very careful with it. Note that there are some who DO crush it with paid reputation leads. Radio, bus benches, billboards, and sponsoring things can be ego plays more than they are actionable plays. Spending your way to the top is a dangerous game. It takes intentional strategy in order to maximize those mediums and will only be effective if there are many sturdy bricks already laid on your foundation.

2
The Hatch Model Blueprint

We've spent the first half of this book discussing the key concepts - the why. Now we get into the nitty gritty of how. The purpose of this blueprint is to outline how to build a team in a sustainable, intentional way. You get the benefit of learning from our mistakes as well as our hard-fought victories. Whereas Section 1 had chapters, Section 2 will have tiers. Each tier describes a developmental level of the agent, charting the career from start to eventual finish. We want to stress right off the bat that there is no one-size-fits-all approach, and this needs to be customized to your specific skills, talents, and team. But this blueprint is a start, an outline of what the future of your business could look like.

First things first - let's take a look at all of the cornerstones that make up a real estate business. **Selling homes is the foundation of all we do**. On top of that, you'll find four unique pillars that make up all of the different categories of expertise one should focus on to build a sustainable business. These are **leadership, support, lead conversion, and marketing**. There are a plethora of key hires you can make to build out your business, but where to start? Don't you worry - we got you! Our Hatch Model Blueprint will show you step by step who you need to hire and when.

LEADERSHIP	SUPPORT	LEAD CONVERSION	MARKETING
Human Relations	Listing Coordinator	Inside Sales Agent (ISA)	Graphic Design
Recruiter	Transaction Coordinator	Database Manager	Marketing Manager
Sales Manager	Executive Assistant	ISA Partner	Photography
Broker	Accounting & Bookkeeping		Videography
Chief Executive Officer (CEO)	Stager		Social Media Expert
Chief Operations Officer (COO)	Reception & Front Desk		Past Client/SOI Coordinator
Chief Financial Officer (CFO)	Office Manager		Event Coordinator
Chief Cultural Officer (CCO)	Runner		
Chief Technology Officer (CTO)			
Training & Development			

SALES
- Buyer Agent
- Listing Agent
- Agent
- Negotiator
- Showing Partner
- Listing Partner

As you build out your team, knowing the specific responsibilities and tasks tied to your real estate business is going to be absolutely imperative. Use the graphics below as a guide to empower your team members as well as to inspect if you're covering all aspects of your business. There are 121 different areas of responsibility within a well-run real estate business. It's hard to specialize when we have to generalize. That's the beauty of growing a team. The bigger you get, the less hats you have to wear!

SALES RESPONSIBILITIES

- Lead generate
- Lead follow-up
- Role play daily
- Nurture past clients and sphere of influence

BUYERS
- Meet with potential buyers
- Get buyers under contract
- Obtain pre-approval/pre-qualification for financing
- Set buyers up on searches
- Manage expectations
- Show buyers homes
- Service buyers
- Obtain estimations of closing costs
- Manage timelines of buyers and sellers
- Research and communicate all fees, taxes, etc. on potential properties
- Write offers for buyers
- Negotiate contracts for buyers
- Attend home inspections & any additional consults with buyers
- Negotiate appraisals
- Communicate with buyers during the escrow period
- Attend the final walk thru
- Attend closing

SELLERS
- Meet with potential sellers
- Prepare CMA
- Visit & evaluate the property
- Get sellers under contract
- Provide seller net sheet
- Stage/consult the presentation of the home
- Manage timelines of buyers and sellers
- Communicate weekly with sellers
- Hold open house(s) for sellers
- Negotiate contracts for sellers
- Coordinate and negotiate inspection
- Negotiate appraisal
- Communicate with sellers during the escrow period
- Attend closing

35 Job Responsibilities

www.hatchcoaching.com

LEADERSHIP RESPONSIBILITIES

HUMAN RELATIONS - hiring, growth, and recruitment

- Placing ads for hiring
- Screening/interviewing candidates
- Handling onboarding and orientation
- Getting team members under contract
- Set and maintain goals
- Conducting regular one on ones
- Attending weekly leadership meetings
- Helping navigate inevitable hurdles (i.e. agents leaving)
- Cast vision
- Lead the leaders
- Coach the team
- Establish the mission, vision, and values
- Schedule and implement pattern interrupts
- Activate involvement in the community
- Handle client complaints
- Review all numbers weekly
- Mastermind with other high-producing agents
- Research market trends and happenings
- Keep all licenses current and active

TRAINING

- Train agents regularly
- Develop and implement onboarding processes
- Lead role play
- Regularly update & innovate the training and onboarding program

25 Job Responsibilities
(3 HR jobs combined into 1)

www.hatchcoaching.com

SUPPORT RESPONSIBILITIES

- Listing coordinating
- Prep contracts
- Input listing into the MLS
- Coordinate photos
- Coordinate staging
- Get feedback from showings
- Communicate weekly with sellers
- Arrange for sign install/removal
- Install/remove sign
- Master and run systems
- Maintain archives
- Keep the office fully stocked and organized
- Schedule events and meetings
- Handle building maintenance and upkeep
- Manage the P&L
- Make deposits
- Pay bills
- Manage bookkeeping
- Prepare tax filings and payments
- Set up contract-to-closing file
- Fill out the CDA (commission disclosure agreement)
- Coordinate necessary paperwork with all involved vendors, clients, and realtors
- Arrange for closing services
- Communicate necessary dates and times with all parties
- Coordinate appraisals
- Prepare for state audits of real estate transactions
- Manage all IT - printers, scanners, computers, internet, servers, firewall, security
- Manage office email accounts and calendars
- Manage benefits, payroll, taxes, unemployment, etc.

29 Job Responsibilities

www.hatchcoaching.com

LEAD CONVERSION RESPONSIBILITIES

- ISA support and guidance
- Organize database
- Initiate conversation with leads
- Follow up with long-term prospects
- Turn leads into appointments for agents
- Ensure lead coverage time from 8 a.m. to 9 p.m. every day of the year
- Respond to all leads within five minutes
- Respond in a timely manner to leads that text back (within an hour or so)
- Answer calls from leads and unknown numbers
- Monitor set appointment to ensure agents execute the intro text/updating notes
- Often take customer and other agent complaints since they call the office
- Lead spend monitoring and adjusting
- Agent lead audits
- Serving as the liaison between the company and lead sources
- Hold agents accountable for dropped balls
- Create and implement lead conversion systems

16 Job Responsibilities

www.hatchcoaching.com

MARKETING RESPONSIBILITIES

- Coordinate marketing efforts
- Design marketing materials
- Arrange for necessary marketing partners
- Market listings
- Market the team/culture
- Plan and implement events
- Purchase and coordinate client gifts
- Write/place PR stories
- Design and maintain website
- Photograph listings
- Videography
- Social media posts
- Blog & content writing
- Graphic design
- Capture reviews and testimonials
- SEO management

16 Job Responsibilities

www.hatchcoaching.com

And now, let's dive into the Perfect Real Estate Agent Blueprint!

Tier 1: The New Agent

A career in real estate can be incredibly rewarding, but it can also be riddled with challenges, especially at the beginning. The National Association of Realtors shared a report in 2014 that 87% of new agents left the business for good within the first five years. Simply put, the traditional real estate model just isn't working for most people. Let's examine this a little closer by meeting a fresh-faced and ambitious woman named Carrie.

Note: We will be providing various visual aids throughout these tiers in order to better conceptualize each level. Above, you will see the darkened circle entitled Rainmaker Agent. Below are two subtle admin circles, a showing partner, and an ISA. These roles are on the horizon as the business grows and will be explained in later sections, but they do not yet apply to this particular tier.

THE NEW AGENT: CARRIE

Carrie is a Tier 1 agent. She's a newbie. She may be new to the real estate world, but she's got big dreams for herself and her family. She's feeling an exhilarating mix of excitement, anxiety, and optimism. She's naive and inexperienced, lacking a network within real estate at this point, but she's hopeful. She's been working as a stay-at-home mom for the last five years, and now with her youngest in school, she's looking forward to making a professional name for herself and helping to support her family financially.

So, Carrie jumps in. She's working the 9-5 hustle of all she thinks a real estate agent should do to be successful. She creates a beautiful custom logo, takes headshots, orders business cards, sends a letter to her family and friends, creates a Facebook business page, and joins the local chamber of commerce. She watches real estate-focused YouTube videos and attends a handful of classes at her broker's office.

COMMON TIER 1 PAIN POINTS:

Carrie knows that her initial business will likely come from her sphere, including her close network of friends and family, but she finds herself struggling with the assertiveness to pursue those leads. She doesn't want to transactionalize her sphere and would hate to come off as sales-y to the people she loves most. Then one day when scrolling through social media, her heart sinks as she sees one of her closest friends has chosen to work with another agent. She may be ready to redefine herself as a realtor, but she's realizing that others may not see her that way. To them, she is still that stay-at-home mom. She imagines they're thinking, *"She's such a nice lady, but do I really trust her to buy or sell my home?"*

It's at this point when nose deep in fear and doubt that the vast majority of people drop out or don't make it in real estate. For those of you on your own path in the field of real estate, you may have felt that doubt before. There can be months and months of hopes and bills without a single closing. Sure, a Tier 1 agent may have loved the idea of entrepreneurship and being her own boss, but now in the midst of the stress and responsibility that comes along with entrepreneurship, fear is creeping in. She is the only person she can rely on at this point, and even then, she may have some major questions about her ability to continue on in this line of work. There is no consistent revenue stream, and it's unclear if there is a paycheck coming. So, scarcity and fear can feel like near-constant companions. She may not be operating on a thoughtful budget or with much financial responsibility or security.

Time is the most precious resource for a Tier 1 agent. A major mistake many agents make at this stage is spending too much time on things that don't matter. They can spend a whole week designing their logo when they don't have any solid business yet. Take that as a prime example of poor return on investment (ROI). She will quickly learn that everything has an ROI attached to it - time, money, and even people. A Tier 1 agent is a solopreneur so learning to be the master of her own schedule is crucial.

That's why at Tier 1, everything needs to be focused on **lead generation, lead conversion, and relationships**. Let's imagine that Carrie was not a realtor but a restaurant owner instead. You don't know her well, maybe she's just an acquaintance from high school, and she says, "You really should come to my restaurant. Best food and best service in town, I promise." You may swing by out of the goodness of your heart, but more often than not, you'll remain neutral on it. She's biased. She wants your business. You may easily forget the interaction all together.

But now let's imagine that your best friend Jamie tells you about how incredible Carrie's restaurant is.

Jamie raves about her experience at the restaurant last weekend. She talks about the cool designs on the walls and the delicious caprese salad and sandwich she had. She compliments the staff's friendliness, noting how they were clearly all trained exceedingly well. She tells you she and her family will definitely be returning. You know Jamie. You trust Jamie.

You're much more likely to check it out now because her rave review doesn't seem biased at all. It seems genuine.

Word-of-mouth referrals are key to Tier 1. Instead of focusing on the things that are *not working*, it's crucial to be *networking*. She has nobody to hype her up yet, so she needs to earn that through relationships and service. Now, let's say that your friend Jamie approves of Carrie as an agent. Jamie tells you about it. You intrinsically trust Carrie more because of Jamie's endorsement. We listen to people we trust. Slowly but surely, that word of mouth spreads, and Carrie gains momentum as a trusted agent in town. That identity she sought to establish from the start finally begins to take root.

HATCH MODEL INSIGHT: TIER 1

Erik: I worked in youth ministry before starting out in real estate. I was well known and well respected in the community. People trusted me with their kids and with their emotions. I was naive enough to assume that would translate into them trusting me with their real estate decisions. That was a farce.

I made plenty of mistakes that first year. I remember taking an ad out in a local business magazine for $150. It was essentially my headshot with the words "Erik Hatch: Trusted with all of your real estate needs." My mediocre advertising attempt didn't make the phone ring like I expected. I didn't close a single deal that year.

Forward momentum started when I focused on the **stuff that matters.** Year two, I got intentional about working open houses. I worked listings for other agents on my team. I made sure to be assertive in letting people know I was a realtor. People began referring me to their family and friends, and the snowball of business kept building. That first year, I didn't sell a single home. This last year, I sold over 1,000. The road from zero to 1,000 was a long and winding one, but I learned a lot along the way.

Working a full-time commission job is difficult, and it takes a certain calling to have the gumption to actually go for it. Most realtors fall into at least one of the following categories. **Trust Fund Kid:** You've got mommy or daddy's money to support you through the first few months without the stress of needing to put food on the table. **Sugar Baby:** You've got a sugar daddy or mama to support you through the turbulent first few months. **Working a Second Job:** You're juggling another full- or part-time job while pursuing a real estate career in order to pay the bills. **Poor Financial Habits:** You throw caution to the wind and trust that it'll be okay. That's tomorrow's problem. **Six Months of Living Expenses in a Savings Account:** We say six months or more is ideal, but you should have at least four months minimum in savings. You've planned appropriately and can weather half a year of financial uncertainty without great anxiety or hardship. You've budgeted for it. You don't need to stress.

Cash Reserves

It is recommended that you have cash reserves of at least four months of PERSONAL and BUSINESS expenses in the bank before you make a move to another tier.

With that financial safety net in place, you can eliminate unnecessary stress and really get to work. Joining a team and working as a showing partner is one route that provides an additional layer of support and is something any newbie should consider. We will describe the showing partner role in greater detail later in this book.

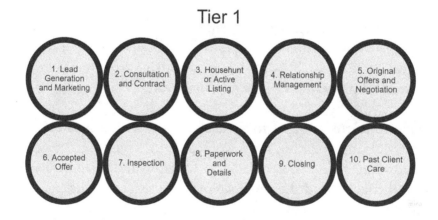

You will see a graph of responsibilities presented at the end of each tier in The Blueprint. The purpose is to help conceptualize which responsibilities fall on the agent's shoulders at any given time. As you see above, all 10 responsibilities are the same shade. This is because throughout Tiers 1 and 2, that person is doing it all, but at the end of Tier 3, you will notice a darker shade in two of the categories. This signifies those responsibilities have either been partially or completely taken off the plate of the agent and given to someone else on the team.

For many, building their business on a real estate team proves to be a wise move. Surround yourself with disciplined individuals and gain the support that's needed.

And if you choose to go about starting your real estate career on your own instead of with a team, you have the option to purchase leads. If you purchase leads this early on, please be warned - it's hard. Way hard. Your skills aren't fully developed, and you don't know what leads will be best for you to convert. Leading with personal business will breed a much more solid foundation.

TIER 1 : "I'm the new kid on the block"

Production #s: 0-10 transactions

Team size: 1

CEO Salary: $0.00

Where should you focus your time?
- Production
- Building your vision
- Growing your database

Pain Points:
- Not enough money coming in
- High Risk of failure
- Feel like a hamster on a hamster wheel
- Lots of running, little results

Solution:
- Focus on your habits
- Get diligent with honoring your schedule and doing the most important things
- Develop yourself & your database, lead generate massively, & deliver a high level of service to your clients
- Work on capturing mindshare that will lead to market-share

New Tools Needed: Free Google Account (Calendar, Email), Marco Polo

Graduation Checklist:
- Averaging one closing per month
- A pipeline of future business
- Some side money saved up to cover basic expenses, a checking account for the business
- Follow your daily schedule

Expected Income (Salary, Production, and Profit):
- No salary
- Earning 30-45% from your personal transactions
- Getting the business to 25% profit +

Tier 2: The One (Wo)Man Band

Tier 2 is similar to Tier 1 in many ways. The agent is still running their business solo, but alas, there is actual business to be had. It's fantastic! Until it's too overwhelming. Tier 2 is all about finding routines and systems that work to keep the business healthy.

THE ONE-MAN BAND: DAVE

Tier 2 agents are a one-man (or one-woman) band. Imagine a musician standing on a street corner, a drum kit strapped to his back, guitar in hand, and harmonica propped up near his mouth. He's trying to do it all - keep the rhythm, sing the melody, and entertain the crowd. He's making it happen, but it's a lot to manage. It can look a bit ridiculous at times. It can get messy. Let's zoom in on Tier 2 agent Dave to see how things are going for him at this stage.

COMMON TIER 2 PAIN POINTS:

The good news for Dave is that business is picking up at this stage. The bad news is he's working so hard keeping up with his right-now business that his tomorrow business is suffering. There are no real tried-and-true systems in place yet, so poor customer service happens pretty regularly. Communication lags, email responses get slower, texts get forgotten about, and phone calls get missed. *He's spending money chasing shiny objects and not on the shit that matters.* He's laser focused on trying to grow, prioritizing his business more than God, family, and himself. The most important people in his world aren't getting the best of him; they're getting what's left of him. He needs to reassess and recalibrate to prioritize what matters. He needs a new plan.

HATCH MODEL INSIGHT: TIER 2

Erik: To be successful at Tier 2, Dave needs to be able to zoom out and see all that needs to get done in a week. He will need to prioritize each of those things in his calendar and in his mind. Each scheduled event is important. Each commitment is valuable and needs to be honored with presence of mind. But wait, *didn't we just say that Dave was a one-man band? How is he suddenly supposed to manage all of those responsibilities? How is any Level 2 agent going to find a balance?*

There are two crucial components at Tier 2: **discipline** and **consistency**. In order to move to Tier 3 and do so with any sense of balance, his days need to be time-blocked and structured in a way that takes an inordinate amount of intention and dedication. To best set himself up for success, **2.5 hours** each morning should be spent on building his business for tomorrow. From 8:30 to 11:00 a.m. each day, he needs to be practicing, lead generating, and planning.

At 11:01, his client-facing activities begin. There isn't one specific path to success in the lead generation game, but it's crucial to be consistent over and over again. When I was just starting out in real estate, I leaned heavily into my SOI (sphere of influence). I had built a huge network of connections from my previous work in youth ministry. With consistent and intentional effort, those connections around the Fargo community were a strong enough foundation to really get the ball rolling for my business. I needed to continue to assess and recalibrate every step of the way. *Is this strategy working? How do I know? What do I need to change?*

Once Dave can check off that initial 2.5 hours of intentional morning tasks, the rest of the day is dedicated to showings, inspections, writing and negotiating contracts, listing appointments, administrative work, and communication. Remember, Dave still wears all of the hats at this point. It's important not to minimize or ignore the monotonous or "unsexy" tasks. Let's say a client is in town and can only do a showing in the morning. Those morning responsibilities do not get canceled or cleared from his schedule; they get moved to the next open time slot. If he has to adjust his schedule, he doesn't remove the unsexy tasks; he needs to reschedule them. Naturally, he will fall off of his routine from time to time, but he needs to have the dedication to get right back on track. Consistency is key. **Over time, unsexy tasks lead to sexy results.**

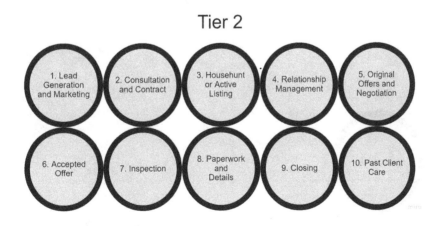

TIER 2 : "I'm starting to figure this out"

Production #s: 11-36 transactions

Team size: 1

CEO Salary: $5,000-$15,000

Where should you focus your time?
- Production
- Building your vision
- Growing your database
- It's time to start the hiring & recruitment process for your 1st admin

Pain Points:
- Each day is stretched thin
- Wearing many hats
- Details bog you down
- Slow to respond & communicate
- Rides a production roller-coaster
- Working 60+ hours per week
- Feels like you can't catch a breath

Solution:
- Hire an admin to start taking transaction work/details off your plate
- This admin is the mess cleaner
- Reinvest most of that time back into lead generation to continue growing your business

New Tools Needed: Google Suite (Calendar, Email), Wizehire

Graduation Checklist:
- Pay yourself a salary
- Following daily schedule
- Selling 20+ homes annually
- Formed an LLC
- Profit numbers are at a green light

Expected Income (Salary, Production, and Profit):
- Collecting a small salary
- Earning 30-45% from your personal transactions
- Getting the business to 25% profit +

Tier 3: Hiring Your First Admin

It's important to note that in Tier 2, agents are working in the business, not *on the business*. The solution to move forward is to hire an admin to take some of those details off of the agent's plate. This is the person that helps you breathe. The process of hiring this person will be the bridge into Tier 3.

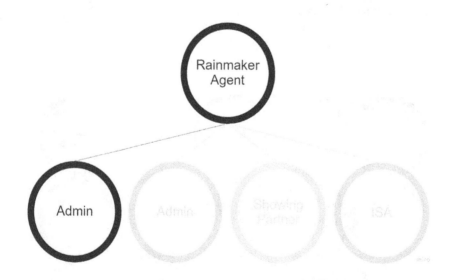

FIRST ADMIN HIRE

Hiring an additional person can feel like an overwhelming decision. But at this point, decision making needs to be logical, not emotional. Do you have steady business and at least 3-4 months of personal and business expenses saved? Have you been paying yourself a salary? Have you formed an LLC? Have you saved for taxes? Are you lead generating for 90 minutes a day? Are you in the range of 20-36 transactions?

Let's meet up-and-coming, goal-oriented Abby. She's met the criteria on that checklist. She has saved like a boss and formed her LLC. She's become a lead-generating machine and is solidly sitting at 34 transactions for the year and counting. It's a natural time for her to transition into Tier 3.

COMMON TIER 3 PAIN POINTS:

Abby's biggest roadblocks as she contemplates making this hire are fear and ego. She's nervous about taking on a salaried employee. Her ego has her convinced that nobody can do it quite like she can. She's got a healthy dose of self-confidence that has helped her succeed so far, but it's showing up as arrogance in assuming she can go it alone. She is acting as though she should be able to do it all and continue to grow. But what Abby doesn't see is her fear and ego are setting her up to implode. This lifestyle is not sustainable. Every agent, no matter how incredible, will reach maximum capacity at some point if they are delivering a high level of service and value. Success breeds growth. There are things that need to be taken off her plate in order to free up more space for the *shit that matters*. If Abby were to follow this blueprint, she could move forward with confidence.

HATCH MODEL INSIGHT: TIER 3

Erik: I remember feeling like Abby. I knew it was time to invest in my business, bet on myself, and hire my first admin. But I was nervous. I was stuck in my fear and ego, thinking about how much pressure it would be to add someone to the payroll. If I failed, it wouldn't only affect me and my wife anymore; it would directly impact that person's livelihood as well which was a gigantic pill to swallow.

When Abby makes the decision to grow her team and make that first hire, it is foremost imperative that she makes the **right hire.** If she doesn't follow the hiring process from Chapter 2, she is leaving herself much more vulnerable to chaos and heartache. Rushing the process and making an impulsive hire without proper consideration and vetting is bound to cause headaches down the line. The final risk is not having a **training process** established. To best prepare this new admin, it's important this person has ample opportunity to watch Abby first. Next, Abby takes intentional time to watch the admin take on those responsibilities, providing feedback and suggestions for improvement as needed. Finally, the admin is trusted to go it alone. We refer to this simply as, *"Watch me. Watch you. Go and do."*

How to Train and Empower Your Team

1. WATCH ME
Shadowing is essential for the new person to see you in action.

2. WATCH YOU
Oftentimes, this is the most skipped-over piece and yet the most important. Taking the time for you to shadow the new person is a cornerstone for success. Do not skip this step! Don't leave this step too quickly, either. Lots of coaching and accountability exist here.

3. GO AND DO
Once they've watched you and you've seen them perform well, they have now earned the right to own the role.

The most important reason for this hire is to allow the agent to focus on income-producing activities as often as possible. The first admin is teeing the agent up, but the agent is still the one hitting the ball. The agent's job as the leader of this newly formed team is to grow the business in a healthy and sustainable way. The newly hired admin's role is to hone in on the more detailed work that helps the business run but isn't necessarily helping to add opportunities for the business to grow. They are the **Systems Master**. They are the transaction coordinator, listing coordinator, office manager, and systems support. It's important for a Tier 3 agent to be clear right off the bat that this role is a real utility player. They may bring the agent's dog to the vet. They may bring the agent's vehicle in for an oil change. Their entire job is to provide leverage so the agent can focus on high dollar-per-hour activities. For a $20/hour investment into them, an agent should be making $100/hour or more with that reinvested time going toward production.

Abby decides to follow the blueprint. She thoughtfully chooses a quality admin to join her business. Her admin has been well trained and is fully capable of removing any minutiae-killing activities. Abby is now able to leverage her time and grow her business without a lengthy list of non-income-producing to dos. She has gotten back 20+ hours in her week and is better able to serve her clients. Abby's business continues to flourish over the next few months, and as it does, she also starts to brainstorm for the future of her business. She's got ideas for marketing strategies, client events, and housewarming gifts. She wants to revamp her social media presence. Abby's got the time for the **ideas** but doesn't quite have the time for the **execution**. This is when Abby needs to start thinking about a move to Tier 4.

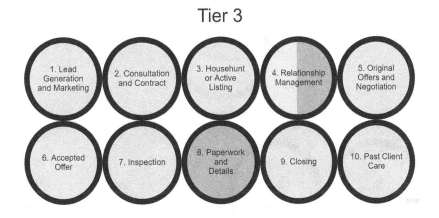

TIER 3 : "I am dropping balls and need an admin"

Production #: 20-55 transactions

Team size: 2

CEO Salary: $10,000 - $20,000

Where should you focus your time?

- Leadership of your admin
- Development of vision
- Production
- Growing your database
- It's time to start the hiring and recruitment process for your 2nd admin

Pain Points:

- 50% increase in clients
- Lack of time to work on the business
- Too many visions for what you want your business to become

Solution:

- Hire a growth-oriented admin who can help take on projects to attract more business
- You will serve as the vision creator, but this person can be your doer

New Tools Needed: Canva, Graphic Design, Group Me/Slack

Graduation Checklist:

- Consistently selling 3+ homes per month
- Admin is properly trained & leveraging things off of your plate
- 4+ months of business & personal expenses in the bank
- Profit numbers are at a green light

Expected Income (Salary, Production, and Profit):

- Collecting a small salary
- Earning 30-45% from your personal transactions
- Getting the business to 25% profit +

Tier 4: Hiring Your Second Admin

Abby's business has continued to grow. She's got plenty of **ideas** but doesn't have enough hours in the day for the **execution**. This is the point at which Abby needs to start thinking about her second admin hire which will move her into Tier 4.

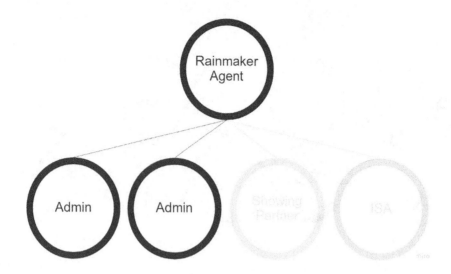

SECOND ADMIN HIRE

As the business continues to grow, both Abby and her admin stay busy. What was once a fairly manageable admin position has now turned into a very full plate, trying to take things off Abby's daily calendar and balance many responsibilities that come along with growing the business. Abby has goals and dreams for the business she wants to pursue, but she sees her admin's stress level growing alongside her list of responsibilities. She's not confident her admin has the capacity to take on any more projects right now. That lack of capacity isn't only time or energy for that first admin; it may even be a lack of the skills needed to take on more creative, forward-thinking pursuits.

Abby has felt the benefits of that first admin hire. She knows it has been a key component to her recent success. She's now at 50 transactions, and her business continues to grow. Her clients are satisfied. Word-of-mouth referrals are helping Abby get consistent quality leads, and she's really proud of the work she's doing. But no matter how much she's accomplishing, that fear and ego she felt before her first hire is still there as she contemplates her second.

COMMON TIER 4 PAIN POINTS:

It's completely natural for Abby to feel hesitant about taking on more financial responsibility. A bit of anxiety can mean she's being truly thoughtful and conscientious about her business and potential employees. But again, it's crucial for any agent contemplating these hires not to make the decision emotionally. This is a numbers game. It's important not to phrase the question, "How much will this cost me?" Here's the real question, "What is my ROI on this?"

HATCH MODEL INSIGHT: TIER 4

Erik: If Robby or I were coaching Abby, we would remind her to keep a 3-to-1 ROI on any hire she makes. Using that rule as her guide, a $40,000/year salaried admin would need 15 more transactions a year at an average commission of $8,000. She, as the rainmaker, is the biggest producer at this stage, so all of the leverage needs to be built around her. If the numbers are there to support an additional hire, it's time to do it.

Return On Investment (ROI)

- It is recommended that everything has a minimum of a 3:1 ROI.
- If you purchase a lead source, you should expect a 3:1 ROI after a recommended six months of that lead source running (and that 3:1 is the company dollar AFTER the split with the agent).
- If you make a hire (an admin at 40k/year, for example), you should be able to track 120k in additional revenue from the leverage they bring. If your average commission is 8k, you would need to sell 15 more houses to justify this person's salary (15 houses x 8k = 120k).

If she does, here's what I would expect to see. Abby gets out of her head, sets down her fear and ego, and runs the numbers. The math supports another hire. She can't deny that in order to get her business where she wants it to go. She needs another person to help get it there. This person is the **Execution of Ideas Master**. Once again, she takes her time with the process, chooses carefully, and trains the person well. That wish list of brainstormed items - client events, housewarming gifts, and the like - can now move from ideas into reality with the time and talent of her second admin. The second admin hire takes over past client plans, community engagement, and marketing. They may also take over Abby's social media, posting on various platforms and creating videos for YouTube or Facebook. Abby understands this person doesn't need to be perfect at content production, maybe only a 6/10, but efficiency is key.

The first admin helped take things off of Abby's plate. The second admin adds things to her plate, but they are things worthy of her time and attention. Marketing, social media, client relations, community engagement - these are the things that keep the business growing and evolving for the better. The first admin helps the business run. The second admin helps the business grow. Both are valuable and help Abby's business continue to thrive.

The Systems Master role (Tier 3) works like an executive assistant. The Executor of Ideas (Tier 4) role works like an assistant executive. It's important to note that after hiring your second admin, you may discover the personalities of these two people you've hired are better suited for the other role. It would be ridiculous to insist that a fish climb a tree just because that's the role they were hired for. Go ahead and place your Tier 4 hire into that systems-focused role and move your Tier 3 hire into the idea-executing role if that is what best utilizes the talents of each person.

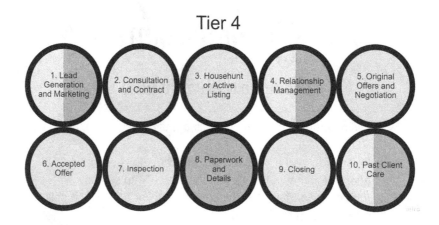

TIER 4 : "I'm ready to grow & another admin is key"

Production #s: 40-70 transactions

Team size: 3

CEO Salary: $10,000-$20,000

Where should you focus your time?
- Leadership of one admin (1 leads the other)
- Continued vision casting
- Production and growing your database
- It's time to start the hiring and recruiting process for your first showing partner

Pain Points:
- Showings & client-facing responsibilities continue to mount
- Your growth is capped due to you being the only agent on your micro-team
- You need another key hire to service your growing business
- You are perhaps out of whack for paying a higher % to salaries but should be paying less for other expenses
- You and your clients deserve better

Solution:
- Hire a partner to come in and join your team (after they get their real estate license) to assist with the servicing of your clients
- This team member serves as the nurse to you serving as the doctor

New Tools Needed: CRM, transaction management software, website

Graduation Checklist:
- Consistently selling 4+ homes per month
- Both admin are trained & functioning at a high level
- 4+ months of business & personal expenses in the bank
- Profit numbers are at a green light

Expected Income (Salary, Production, and Profit):
- Collecting a small salary
- Earning 30-45% from your personal transactions
- Getting the business to 25% profit +

Tier 5: A Crossroads

It is in Tier 5 where you find yourself at a crossroads - do you stay small and mighty, utilizing your admin support only? Or is it time to add a "producer" or two? What if we told you that adding a producer is the wrong step?

The showing partner model is a fairly new concept in the world of real estate, and for that reason, resistance to it can be expected. Lack of information about or exposure to this model is usually at the core of that resistance.

Showing partners differ from the typical agent in that they often have a guaranteed salary. This means they can weather those first few months with less financial anxiety. They're provided mentorship to help them learn tried-and-true systems to increase efficiency and built-in accountability to keep them growing. There's less pressure to perform instantly, so they are able to focus on the job at hand without the added pressure, desperation, and fear that comes along with a scarcity mindset. This model is different, and different is hard for people. Let's take a look at Tony as he contemplates which direction he will go to grow his team.

THE TIER 5 CROSSROADS

Tony is a successful agent with two admin on his team. He's ready to take on the next chapter in his business, make more money, and free up time in his life. The traditional real estate growth model for people like Tony has been: *Go grow your team and get out of production. Add people to your ecosystem! Hire an additional buyer agent, maybe even two agents, and you'll sell more homes.* That's the fantasy but not always a reality.

Let's imagine Tony is at a crossroads on his walk toward successful team growth. He stands at that fork in the road and looks up at a sign with two arrows. Pointing left is an arrow that reads, *The Traditional Model.* The path is well worn. He's heard a lot of rainmakers have traveled that path before him. Pointing right is another arrow that reads, *The Hatch Model.* He sees that path to his right, much less worn, weaving its way around the bend. It looks a lot different than the traditional way. He's nervous about the road less taken.

So, he turns left, choosing the traditional, well-worn path. Tony has five quality leads that he as the agent could and likely would close. Let's say there is a $10k commission for each of these leads. That's $50k if all of them close. But in keeping with that traditional model, he hires a buyer agent to join his team. This new buyer agent, Hannah, will get 50% of the commission on those deals. Tony will get 50% of the commission. Tony assumes he will get $25,000 easily without having to lift a finger. But once again, this is pure fantasy.

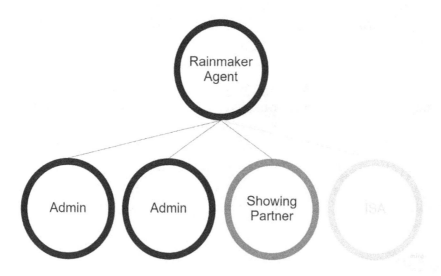

COMMON TIER 5 PAIN POINTS:

Anyone who has led a team could tell Tony that's not how it will play out. Sure, Tony himself could close those five deals, but Hannah is poorly trained and inexperienced. She may convert three out of the five at best. She will make $15k, and Tony will make $15k over the course of two months. Even more realistically, Hannah will only convert two of the five. She will get $10k, and Tony will get $10k. Now, Hannah will need to wait 4-to-6 months to get paid. She may be feeling broke, stressed, and anxious, maybe even starting to question if this is the right fit for her. She may need to pick up a second job to pay the bills in the meantime which then affects her ability to provide adequate customer service to her clients which in turn leads to even less lead conversion. Hannah is now a flight risk, and who could blame her? Yet we wonder why this model is broken.

The buyer agent isn't the problem. **The model is the problem.** This traditional path to team growth yields inconsistent results. Over 80% of realtors don't make it past their first few years. These agents are often undertrained and underdeveloped. Rainmakers hand them crumbs, leftovers, and mediocrity - the leads that haven't been adequately nurtured, and these new, green agents are expected to magically convert. This is a lose/lose/lose situation. The buyer agent loses because they were ill equipped with crappy leads and little support. The client loses because they receive subpar customer service. And the rainmaker loses too because he's losing time and money. He will go through the hiring and training process again and again because this model doesn't create an ecosystem to grow and maintain a healthy team.

Tony is stumbling and struggling on the traditional path. He walks back to the fork in the road and looks up at the arrows. Pointing right, he once again sees *The Hatch Model*. He decides he's ready to try this new way. So, he sets out on the lesser-worn trail, both nervous and excited about what's to come for him and his team.

HATCH MODEL INSIGHT: TIER 5

Erik: Tony needs to move Hannah into the position of **showing partner**. She now becomes a salaried employee and trains under his leadership. Tony may still be the "doctor," but now Hannah is the "nurse" on those deals. Tony is the one negotiating and doing the heavy lifting, but the day-to-day nurturing and client contacts are now Hannah's responsibilities. She handles the showings and communication which frees up Tony's time to focus on the operations, strategizing, and game planning. Hannah handles the nurturing of clients so they feel seen, heard, and valued throughout the entire process. Tony pays Hannah $3,000/month for this showing partner role. That's $6k over two months that Tony has invested into Hannah, but Hannah will do about 70-80% of the day-to-day responsibilities when it comes to those five leads. And when those leads convert into closed deals, Tony gets to keep $50k, invests the 6k into Hannah's 2-month salary, a net positive of $44k. He has nearly tripled his return by choosing this new path.

It's important to hone in on the language used when we talk about this role. This person is not your showing *assistant*. An assistant makes it sound as if a client is being handed off to someone who doesn't pack quite the same amount of punch you do, and that's not the case. **A partner is first and foremost responsible for leveraging your time as the lead agent**. They are an extension of you. In the client's mind, that small difference matters.

The second responsibility of this partner is to train diligently. They focus on role play, developing themselves, practicing, and getting better. Your focus with this person is to build them up and train them in such a way that makes them exceptional.

When I was initially forming my team, that's where the list of responsibilities ended for this partner role. These partners would leverage my time and continue to train for excellence, and then 12 months later, they would graduate into an agent role. But let's remember that everything should be earned, and nothing should be given. I quickly learned it was necessary for these partners to bring in their own sphere, open house leads, and referrals. **The final responsibility of these partners needs to be lead generation.** When they take on that additional layer of investment in the business, you'll discover these partners are paying for themselves.

Showing Partner Financial Breakdown

Example:
Average commission of $8,000
Showing partner salary of $32,000
Agent split: 40%
Average agent commission: $3200 (40% of $8,000)
# of deals a showing partner has to add to your bottom line to break even: 10

- The showing partner will be buying you back a plethora of time as they take much off your plate. Your newfound time is best invested into deepened lead conversion and lead follow-up.
- The showing partner should be adding a number of transactions to your bottom line from their sphere, open houses, and company-converted leads.

In order to justify the addition of a showing partner in the Fargo market, an agent would need to sell approximately 10 additional houses in a year. But what we have found with our Hatch Model is when a showing partner is added, an agent ends up with about 15-25 more houses/year on average. These partners are often bringing in an additional $50-60k for the agent in a year just by adding that lead generating responsibility to their to-do list. For any deal a partner brings in from their own sphere or lead generation, it is recommended the agent pay them a 15% cut on that deal. The typical 25% referral rate would not be necessary because lead generation is part of their salaried responsibilities. These showing partners are **gold**.

SHOWING PARTNER

ROLES: (ordered by importance)
- Leverage the agent (this can include a multitude of personal and professional tasks)
- Train and role play regularly
- Lead generate

RESPONSIBILITIES:
- Shows homes to clients
- Attends inspections & final walk-throughs on behalf of agent
- Proactively house hunts for the clients
- Maintains communication with clients throughout the home hunting process

COMPENSATION:
- 30-40k/year + salary (depending on your market)
- 5% of gross commission on the deals they helped service (this is optional) - paid by the agent
- 15% commission on any deals they procure through their own efforts

RECOMMENDATIONS:
- Showing partner is highly recommended when you start selling 30+ homes/year
- Your partner may help with other duties beyond what is stated
- A partner's purpose is to leverage your time so you can focus on high dollar-producing activities

3 Main Jobs for a Showing Partner (in this order):

1. Leverage their agent
This includes showings, client connections, some admin work, inspections, runner duties, personal leverage needs, and any other piece that helps keep the agent in high $/hr activities.

2. Train and develop
Your partner is your future "starter" in your lineup, and the development of them is crucial.

3. Lead generate
Part of their graduation requirements should be their ability to feed themselves by showing competency and consistency in capturing business for tomorrow.

Whereas the traditional path resulted in a lose-lose-lose, this new path is producing a win-win-win. Tony is no longer giving his best opportunities to a very green and ill-equipped Hannah. He is closing those deals and keeping the commissions. He's able to leverage his business and his life. Meanwhile, Hannah is essentially earning her MBA from a top agent on how things are done the right way. She's working under Tony's direct leadership and supervision of a skilled and experienced veteran in this field.

That **proximity** is priceless. She is provided opportunities to learn and develop without the financial stress and uncertainty weighing on her shoulders. When the time comes for her to transition into an agent role herself, she will do so as a better trained and equipped agent than others in the field. Finally, the client wins big in this model as well. They get constant touches and accessibility from a great showing partner while also having the lead agent's wealth of knowledge and experience at their disposal. They get the time and talents of both professionals to help them score a home they love. Win-win-win.

Getting clear on what value you'll provide a showing partner (or agent, for that matter) is essential. A leader should provide a hefty amount of leads, leadership, and leverage. And it is your leadership that will be the difference between flight risks and those massively dedicated to your ecosystem.

The Value Teams Should Provide:
Leads
Leadership
Leverage

Within the showing partner model, you'll find there are three types of partners: The Lifer, The Graduate, and The Empire Builder. Let's break them down.

HATCH HINT

There are three paths for your showing partners:

1. ***The Lifer -*** This is someone who loves showing homes & lacks the desire for becoming an agent, nor do they demonstrate the aptitude to serve as your ***empire builder.*** These individuals are built like an admin who loves people and interaction.
2. ***The Graduate -*** This is someone who earns the ability to serve as an agent by creating opportunities from their lead conversion efforts. It is imperative to have standards for graduation.
3. ***The Empire Builder -*** They are drawn to the stability provided by getting fed regularly yet have the capacity and skill set to lead and negotiate all details of the transaction.

1. **The Lifer** – This person doesn't want the stress of full-time commissions. They love building relationships and selling homes. They don't mind the lifestyle of some nights and weekends. They may be a little more emotionally attached to the process than other partners, more sensitive to the harsh negotiation process that goes along with selling homes. They may be designed like an admin in some ways, thriving on structure and routine, but they may also appreciate having some freedom and flexibility within their schedule too.

    a. This person is not typically one who is going to be bringing in 10 sphere deals or more annually, but they are extremely valuable. **They are a stabilizer.** They are steady and reliable.

    b. People do not often raise their hand and admit to being The Lifer, but it is crucial that we stress the value in this type of partner. They may not be pushing you forward, but they aren't requiring you to pull them along either. You can count on them to be sitting right beside you, working their tail off and helping you row the boat.

2. **The Graduate** – Most people in a partner role will say they want to be in this camp. On the Hatch team, people stay in the partner role for a **minimum** of one year before graduating to what is called a partner plus, meaning they are representing their own sphere but are still fully salaried and remain in that role for an additional year. These partners need to do a minimum of 20 sphere or referral deals over this minimum 2-year period before graduating to an agent role. It is important to note that Hatch Realty's standards are exceedingly high, and many of our coaching clients modify these standards down to one year and 10 sphere/referral deals to graduate. Though the standards are subject to change based on the needs of your team, it's recommended to never set the bar lower than that 12 months/10 deals benchmark.

a. Graduating out of a partner role happens three ways. 1) They earn it. They have met the requirements set and have proven competency to take on agent responsibilities. 2) Someone leaves. You lose a high-producing agent and need to move your bench player up to the starting lineup. 3) You have so much business, you can't help but move this person up to help with those opportunities.

3. **The Empire Builder** – Let me tell you a not-so-funny story about how I lost over two million dollars in the last seven years by not choosing The Empire Builder route. Here's how it happened … the year was 2013. I personally sold 1,453 homes while leading my team. The next year, 2014, I managed to close 149 homes. I was a machine, working 90-110 hours a week. I was representing a builder at the time so about 50 deals a year were coming from that partnership, but 100 deals a year were coming from my own sphere. By the time 2020 came around, I had only 36 sphere referrals for the year. I continue to see diminishing returns on my sphere business each year. I lost out on 64% of the opportunities in the last seven years.

   Why? Because in October of 2014, I decided to get out of production with the birth of my first child. I decided I wanted to be the engaged and devoted dad that I never had. I chose my family and have never regretted that choice. But what I do regret is how I did it.

   I handed the baton off to other agents on my team, and now, most of those agents aren't with me anymore. What I failed to recognize at the time was that by handing those agents the batons, I was also handing them the relationships. I was being entirely truthful when I would say to my sphere, people like the Johnsons, "You're going to be working with Emily; she's fantastic. She's going to take amazing care of you guys." But in so many ways, I also said, "I can't be your realtor anymore." So, when it came time for the Johnsons to list their home years later, they didn't reach out to me. I had given the relationship away when I gave away the transaction. The Johnsons contacted Emily, and Emily was no longer with the team. That kind of scenario played out over and over and over again with me losing out on $2 million (and counting).

   I wanted to hand off the transaction, but I failed to systemize the relationship first. I didn't stay in close contact with those clients. I failed to acknowledge that agents don't stay with you forever and those relationships with clients aren't going to tend to themselves. I needed to find a system to keep them in proximity - texts or phone calls or Facebook notifications or Marco Polos. I needed to nurture my sphere to keep it. But instead, I learned a $2 million lesson the hard way.

   The Empire Builder shows up as a Graduate, but they don't graduate off your micro team. **They graduate up your team.** So, instead of handing graduating agents a baton to start their own race, The Empire Builder path allows for this race to stay a well-oiled relay within your team. They are now the relationship builder and the negotiator. The agent/rainmaker can now invest deep into the relationship because the transaction is in the hands of The Empire Builder. This gives The Empire Builder a big life because they don't have to be aggressive hunters for business and they get a consistent stream of business from the lead agent/rainmaker while also making six figures. This Empire Builder also gets the benefits of proximity and opportunity built on a strong foundation of leadership.

Why would someone want to be an Empire Builder?

1) Predictable business
2) Proximity to the rainmaker
3) Less risk with still big rewards
4) Prefers deeper versus wider

For each of my deals, this agent is now getting 15% for running/leading/facilitating the transaction. They're the point person, and I'm not involved with their buy or sell.. With their own sphere, they're earning 40%. If I would have hired an Empire Builder, I wouldn't have to touch the transaction but would still benefit greatly from the financial opportunities presented. The Empire Builder ends up making a very comfortable $125-175k/year income in the Fargo market, and they don't have to be hunters. They are gatherers. In higher-priced markets like Denver, Empire Builders are making 250-300k annually.

If I were to do it all over again, I would bring on an Empire Builder instead of giving relationships away to agents. I could say with confidence that by keeping those relationships close to the chest, I would still be doing 100 sphere deals/year (if not more) which would have translated into so much money and opportunity over time.

Types of Showing Partners

1. Lifer
- Base pay of 30-40k
- 5% off of every deal they touch
- 15% from their SOI deals
- Expected annual pay: $60,000 - $80,000

2. Graduate
- Base pay of 30-40k
- 15% from their SOI deals
- Expected annual pay: $40,000 - $60,000
- Once they've earned the right to graduate: $100,000+

3. Empire Builder
- 30-40% from their SOI deals
- 15% from every deal they negotiate successfully for the lead agent
- Expected annual pay: $100,000 - $150,000+

The greatest way to **quick** wealth in real estate is not to build the team; it's for you as the lead agent to sell a lot of houses. Building a team that functions without you on a day-to-day basis is the long-term goal for many. Yet rushing to this has left most team leaders making less and doing more. It's inevitable that some agents will leave for other pursuits, but I wish I would have developed an Empire Builder early on to increase the likelihood they would have stayed on and worked side by side with me to build that empire together.

THE HATCH MODEL BLUEPRINT

HATCH HINT

3 Ways to Create Buy-In with the Showing Partner Model

1. *Go through the four stages of a showing partner.* If possible, we recommend starting at stage two or three.
2. *As the rainmaker, adopt the showing partner model yourself.* This demonstrates the additional opportunities created through the leverage of the showing partner model.
3. *Subsidize the cost of the showing partner with a definitive end date.* When necessary, pay half of the showing partner salary for six months with a ramp down by the end of one year.

1. RENT A PARTNER
- Agents use the showing partner when they are double booked
- $25-$30/hr (depending on your market)

What we've seen: Agents rarely utilize the rent a partner model.

2. SHARE A PARTNER
- Two agents share cost burden of one showing partner & they split showing partner's time
- Base salary of 30-40k

What we've seen: Agents get frustrated because one agent inherently uses showing partner more.

3. MINI TEAM MODEL
- Agents work directly with one showing partner to leverage their business
- Showing partner does nearly all showings, inspections, final walk-throughs, etc.
- Agent focuses on lead gen & contract negotiations
- Base salary of 30-40k + 5% of gross commission (this is optional)

What we've seen: This is the ideal model to scale your business.

4. EMPIRE BUILDER
- Showing partner graduates up and starts taking on your contract negotiations
- Showing partner pay/income increases
- Agent focuses on lead gen & relationship building
- 15% of gross commission

What we've seen: This allows rainmakers/agents to retain connection with their sphere of influence.

Adding a partner has proven to be the most profitable, sustainable, kick-butt win/win/win if you're wanting to grow into a business you aren't glued to at every turn. The partner model is freedom or at least the start of what will be freedom in terms of both finances and time. The move to hire a partner will change the course of your business forever.

One can choose to add additional partners to leverage your business too! Some of the top micro teams are operating with 2-3 partners to support the lead agent.

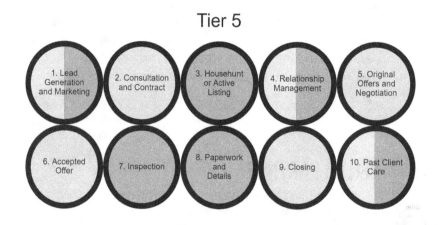

TIER 5 : "Time to add a licensed partner"

Production #s: 60-100 transactions
Team size: 4
CEO Salary: $10,000-$25,000

Where should you focus your time?
- Leadership of one admin (one leads the other)
- Leading your partner
- Continued vision casting
- Production
- Growing your database
- Your time with production is spent lead converting, getting clients under contract, and negotiating deals
- You are a full-time producer and a full-time leader here
- Your admin leverages most of the support work and your partner leverages the day-to-day points of transactions
- It's time to start the hiring and recruitment process for your 1st ISA

Pain Points:
- Production has increased
- Your time is now being devoured by more transactions
- You are spending more money and only picking off the low-hanging fruit because of a lack of database management & masterful lead follow-up systems
- Salaries may still be out of whack with the budget model

Solution:
- Hire a full-time, in-house ISA to start chasing your purchased leads for you
- This person follows up with your long-term prospects, organizes the database, holds you and others accountable, and assesses the conversion rate of your lead sources

New Tools Needed: None

Graduation Checklist:
- Selling 6+ homes per month
- Showing partner is leveraging your business at a high level
- 4+ months of business & personal expenses in the bank
- Purchasing a steady flow of leads (mostly long-term nurtures)
- Invested in a CRM with texting capabilities
- Profit numbers are at a green light

Expected Income (Salary, Production, and Profit):
- Collecting a moderate salary
- Earning 30-45% from your personal transactions (while paying the salary of the showing partner from your personal side & possibly 5% of your commission)
- Getting the business to 25% profit +

Tier 6: Adding an ISA

Lead generation is one thing, but lead conversion is a whole other monster. There are various ways to go out and purchase more leads, but agents in Tier 6 don't typically have a lead generation issue; they have a lead conversion issue. Tier 6 is going to focus on building an ISA department to consistently convert quality leads to strengthen the entire ecosystem of a business.

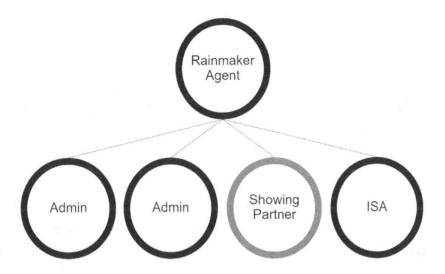

HIRING AN ISA

Let's look to Michelle as an example. Michelle has been leading a lucrative real estate business for the last five years. She's been adding additional admin and showing partners when needed, filling in the gaps and making sure things run smoothly for the *right-now business*. But she and her partners are running into a bad habit time and time again. A new lead comes in for someone wanting to both buy and sell. Michelle writes it on a Post It note to return back to at the end of the day. But the day gets busy, as it always does, and she doesn't have the time to follow up on that lead before she has to run and pick up her kid from basketball practice. She will address it tomorrow. But tomorrow is the same rat race with time and energy spent nurturing the right-now business. Consequently, the tomorrow business falls by the wayside, and agents like Michelle lose out on $20k or more each time because of it. Entrusting lead generation and lead conversion to agents means this full-time need is only getting part-time attention.

It's time for Michelle to increase spending and hire an Inside Sales Agent (ISA). Nurturing the *have-not-mets* requires a kind of time and attention that Michelle and her partners are not able to provide. Michelle has to be humble enough to admit that she and her current team are not equipped to do it all themselves. If they are great with clients and sales, it's a fallacy to assume they should also automatically be great at pursuing and following up on leads. **This isn't an agent issue. This is a systems issue**. Long-term nurtures and touches require a very specific skill set and an enormous time commitment.

COMMON TIER 6 PAIN POINTS:

Michelle may be an incredible agent. She may have a great team. She may have the very best of intentions to follow up with every lead that comes in. But if she's juggling too many balls, some are inevitably going to drop. **Good intentions aren't enough**. Those long-term nurtures and incoming leads need quick responses, structured follow up, and intense dedication. A Post It note from a week ago isn't going to cut it. Even a mediocre ISA is better than a great agent juggling too many balls, because **imperfect action beats inaction every single time**.

Though a mediocre ISA is better than no ISA at all, finding a *great* ISA may be the hardest hire you will ever make. An ISA, in their purest form, is an insurance policy for purchased leads. There is often a misconception that this position is a call center or virtual assistant type, a person solely responsible for responding to leads. But the ISA role is so much more specific and crucial than that and deserves intentional thought and planning to find the right fit.

The role of an ISA is to take incoming leads and put them on the right plans to yield results. These are no longer the Phone Ninjas they used to be in movies like *Boiler Room, Wolf of Wall Street,* or *Glengarry Glen Ross.* There's no longer a need to smile and dial until you fall over. Dials aren't completely dead yet, but the world for the ISA has changed and progressed in such a way that texting is far more valuable and lucrative. We've found that nearly 70% of people won't pick up a phone call but will respond to a text. This means that these ISAs may be ghosted in text form, but they're not receiving the f-offs and insults over the phone that used to be commonplace. This means you no longer need only the thickest-skinned people in this role. That being said, a thick skin doesn't hurt.

Sure, you could go out and hire someone through a third-party company, maybe across the country or even overseas, but what you're getting there is nothing more than a filter to identify the most valuable leads and eliminate the junk. An ISA doesn't just filter out junk. We estimate that to be about 30% of the job. They also connect with leads, build trust with potential clients and agents, foster accountability within teams, and continually improve upon systems for the business to optimize efficiency and improve conversion rates. An ISA will not only take the lead on the right now opportunities but also position themselves to convert the long-term plays. This can be the "Give me a call back in half a year and we'll talk" follow-ups or even the "No, I was just looking for fun." **A good ISA knows that a "no" isn't really a "no" – it's a "not yet."**

HATCH MODEL INSIGHT: TIER 6

Erik: The strongest ISA game is a local ISA game - someone who understands the cultural norms, geography, neighborhoods, and what local people are going through. An in-house ISA can also provide a level of accountability with agents that would be almost impossible to replicate with an outside third party. Accountability requires trust. Trust requires rapport, reliability, and connection. People don't want to take feedback from someone they don't know, trust, or respect. That level of connection is best fostered within your own unique ecosystem.

It's important to note this role is not designed to be a stepping stone to an agent role; it requires a very different skill set than those of most agents. This person needs to know right away that they will never have anything resembling a 9-5 schedule. They will routinely be working nights and weekends. They will be stepping away from family dinners. They will be going into another room to follow up on a lead in the middle of a wedding dance. Their spouse will be driving on the family road trip so they can spend that time chasing leads. Additionally, it takes someone with an inordinate amount of steadfastness to keep pushing through many layers of rejection to succeed in this position.

The way you find and retain this person is by providing a healthy compensation matched with leadership and responsibility. A common compensation model throughout the industry is a small base salary with a commission split on each deal they procure for the team who closes. For example, this could be a base salary of $2,500/month and a 10% commission cut on their closed deals with the commission cut coming directly out of the agent's split.

ISA Compensation

- When licensed, 8-10% of the GCI should be paid to the ISA. This is a deduction from the agent's commission.

  Example (if the agent receives a split of 45%):
  - $10,000 commission
  - 55% to company - $5500
  - 10% to ISA - $1,000
  - 35% to buyer agent - $3500

- When not licensed, (Robby to provide this info) compensation should be

When you hire an ISA, it's important to return to the motto of, "Everything is earned, and nothing is given." This person will need to earn those leads, both to prove to themselves what they are capable of and to earn the respect of the team.

How to Pay an ISA
- Sales price = 250k
- Commission rate = 3%
- Total commission = $7500

*If agent is at a 50/50 split:
Company = 50% - $3750
Agent = 40% - $3000
ISA = 10% - $750

There are five levels of lead generation an ISA will move through as they mature in skills and experience. They begin by scraping their way through old nurture leads and eventually climbing up the ladder to earn access to the highest-quality, come-list-me leads. This proven system will help develop that hire into a skilled ISA, capable of consistently generating and converting quality leads and inevitably earning the respect and appreciation of the whole team.

ISA Onboarding Graduation Tiers

Tier One - Old Nurture Leads
Tier Two - Old Low-Hanging Fruit
Tier Three - New Nurture Leads
Tier Four - New Low-Hanging Fruit
Tier Five - New Come List Me's and Come Buy Me's

Graduation from one level to another requires either 10 appointments set or 100 follow ups created.

The recommended DiSC profile of an ISA is a D-C or a C-D. ISAs should have the ability to be direct, assertive, and authoritative (DiSC profile D). Additionally, they need to be analytical and good with numbers and processes (DiSC profile C). We used to caution people about hiring anyone with a high S in the ISA role. That high S means a person values structure, consistency, and predictability. Those high S qualities can show up in things like hesitancy to make phone calls, fearing they may be disrupting or annoying someone. But now we recognize that people with a high S can find success in an ISA role as long as they do not have that hesitation to interrupt someone's world. The one DiSC profile we would recommend not hiring for this role is a high I. Their needs for connection, influence, and social interaction are not going to be met through ISA responsibilities. Most of an ISA's work will be done alone in text chains, phone calls, emails, and systems, but rarely face-to-face with people.

But the DiSC profile isn't everything. Michelle will need to carefully consider other factors when making this crucial hire. She will need to find someone who is incredibly hungry and patient because seeds planted in lead generation can take a long time to bear fruit. She will need someone who can communicate clearly through written word (texts, emails) and who is both tech savvy and socially savvy enough to adjust that communication to meet the needs of the lead they're talking to.

Robby was the second ISA I ever hired, and quite frankly, he gave a less than stellar interview. He dropped an f-bomb more than once. But his hunger was undeniable, so I took a shot on him. Robby has a D-C DiSC profile, incredibly direct and assertive, data-centered, and analytical, but what made him successful in that role was more personal. He was a broke 23-year-old college graduate with a baby on the way. He was passionate and driven to build a good life for himself and his family. He wanted to make an impact, and his *why* was his fuel through every bit of rejection along the way. Robby became one of the best lead converters in the country and is now the best coach in the country for it. That was possible because of his hunger and his patience.

Michelle needs to find her Robby. Why now? Because her finances support the additional hire and the company is missing out on leads due to a lack of immediacy. She needs to relieve herself and her partners of the things they're not good at or they no longer have the time to do with fidelity. She needs to hire an ISA because leads deserve to be met with timeliness, curiosity, consistency, and dedication that a well-trained ISA can provide.

THE PERFECT REAL ESTATE AGENT BLUEPRINT

Tier 6

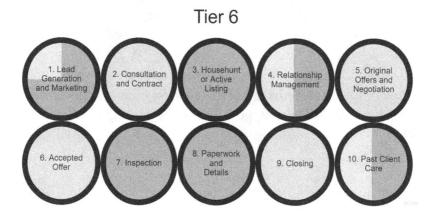

TIER 6 : "Increase spending and hire an ISA"

Production #s: 72-125 transactions

Team size: 5

CEO Salary: $15,000-$30,000

Where should you focus your time?

- Leadership of one admin (one leads the other)
- Leading your partner
- Leading your ISA
- Continued vision casting
- Production
- Growing your database
- Time spent with getting clients under contract and negotiating deals
- Your lead gen is spent on PCSOI
- Full-time producer & full- time leader
- *Admin* - support work, *ISA* - handles lead conversion & have-not-mets, *Partner* - leverages your daily task work
- You are now buying much more business for other agents while also training them
- With more leads coming in, you need to grow your ecosystem with more talent.
- It's time to decide if you want to stay as a micro team or grow to a medium or mega team
- And with that comes more hiring and recruiting

Pain Points:

- Team members are growing in knowledge & talent which means customization of everything is looming
- This will take some serious time & energy
- Salaries are still out of whack if your avg commission is lower

Solution:

- Customize your team structure
- Decide whether to stay micro or grow to medium or mega team
- Once you make this decision, it comes with a massive shift in your daily responsibilities
- Developing yourself into a leader while adding talent around you is inevitable

New Tools Needed: None

Graduation Checklist:

- Selling 7+ homes per month
- ISA is producing 2+ quality appointments/ business day
- Showing partner is highly trained & growing your world massively
- With the addition of the ISA, you have a plethora of business that will require more hands
- 4+ months of business & personal expenses in the bank
- Profit numbers are at a green light

Expected Income (Salary, Production, and Profit):

- Collecting a moderate salary
- Earning 30-45% from your personal transactions (while paying the salary of partner from your personal side and possibly 5% of your commission)
- Earning 30-45% from ISA set appointments (while paying 10% to the ISA from your personal commission)
- Getting the business to 25% profit +

Tier 7: Choosing Team Size

3 Sizes of Teams:
Micro (2-6 people)
Medium (7-12 people)
Mega (13+ people)

It is here at Tier 7 that a rainmaker needs to get very clear on what it means to grow and customize their business. By no means should this be the first time these questions are being considered. If that's the case, the business is likely floundering by now. There needs to be careful consideration and reassessment every step of the way in order to build a strong foundation.

Tier 7- Micro Team Example

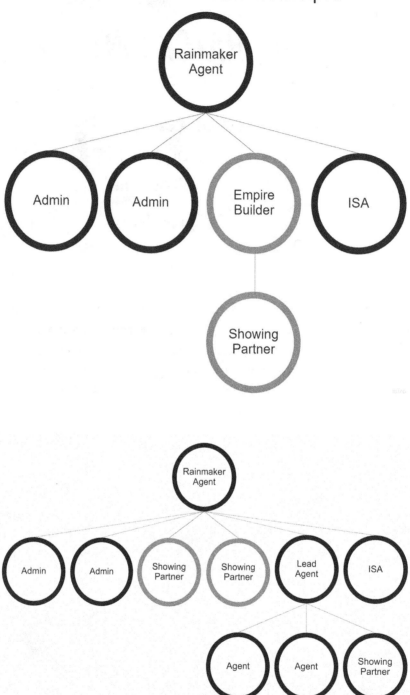

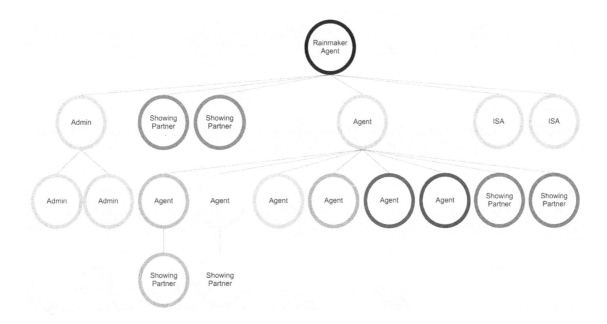

MICRO, MEDIUM, AND MEGA

In order to choose the right path for themselves and their business, it's crucial for a rainmaker to ask themselves, *What gives me joy? What work do I want to avoid? What kind of lifestyle do I want? What are my financial goals? Who do I want to be?* The answers to those questions will be a rainmaker's roadmap as they set out on the next leg of their real estate journey.

There are three broad categories in the world of real estate. **We have coined these as micro teams, medium teams, and mega teams.** It's incredibly tempting to look over your neighbor's fence and think the grass is greener, but it's important to note that no team size is better or worse than the next. Each comes with its own unique set of strengths and potential pain points.

Let's take Trevor as an example. Trevor is the lead agent of a micro team in the Midwest. He works alongside two stellar showing partners, two admin, and an ISA. Because of close proximity and earned trust amongst the team members, decisions are made quickly and without much of a headache. Everyone knows their responsibilities and has become an expert in their designated role. When conflicts occasionally bubble up to the surface, there is enough trust and rapport amongst the team to resolve them fairly quickly.

Trevor is really happy with his micro team. He is financially stable, and his team is reaping the benefits of an efficient, well-oiled machine. That being said, he still carries a lot of responsibility. He's still very much working in the business, not on the business which can be time consuming and draining at times.

He runs into his friend Emma at the Hatch Coaching Summit in Fargo, North Dakota. They catch up over drinks, and she tells him about how her business has really exploded since last spring when she added a second ISA and three buyer agents. For a moment, he feels a tinge of envy in his chest. He knows the potential is there to expand, but he's not confident that's the life he wants.

Fear begins to take root as he listens to Emma's story. When he gets back to his hotel room that night, he wonders what opportunities a medium or mega team could bring. He starts to worry that he may be limiting the potential of his showing partners. He wants to work less and earn more but doesn't want to lose the strong connections within his current micro team. He's not sure that he's built for leadership in the way a medium or mega team would demand, but he sees his friends stepping out of production and thriving while doing so. He thinks about how catastrophic it would be if one of his teammates were to leave, and he envies Emma's ever-growing bench of backups.

But what Trevor doesn't know is that it's not all rainbows and butterflies for Emma either, despite how she made it sound. She's been feeling really pulled in both directions over the last few months between the close intimacy she used to share with her team and the shiny, exciting potential she imagines in a future mega team. When she was leading a team of seven (a nice-sized micro team) before her most recent hires, everyone was well trained, and she felt confident managing her responsibilities as a leader. But her current team of 11 is in the messy middle - an awkward, pimply preteen without much confidence in its identity. She's gone "bigger medium," but now, she either needs to scale down or go mega. Nobody should stay a preteen/messy middle player for long. The consistent pull of production, underdeveloped team members, and leadership leaves Emma wickedly strained.

Emma presents as confident and self-assured, but she's struggling. Her high-I made her great in sales, but she doesn't have the basics of leadership down. Sales is a microwave. She loved that fast-paced lifestyle with exciting days and quick results. But leadership is a crockpot. It lacks that adrenaline and momentum. It's slower. It's more intentional. She knows she needs a coach right now. She reaches out to Erik for support as she contemplates transitioning her business to a mega team.

James is a well-respected and well-known rainmaker on the West Coast. Emma looks to him as an example of leadership she hopes to emulate someday. James has carefully grown his team over the last decade with a current team of 25. He is no longer in the production side of things, focusing instead on the development of producers and leaders on his team. James gives his time and attention to one-on-ones, casting vision, coaching, and leadership development for 10 hours or more each week. He's had to let go of some leadership decisions over the years which was an uncomfortable learning curve at first, but also incredibly necessary.

Here's why – let's imagine James is sitting next to his teenage daughter as she learns to drive. His jaw is clenched, and his shoulders are high. She's going 20 mph in a 45, and he tells her she needs to speed up. She punches the gas, so he tells her to slow down. She grows increasingly overwhelmed and takes a narrow turn, bumping against the curb. He scolds her sarcastically when she does and asks her to pull over. He'll take it from here.

James knew that he could never lead his team that way. He knew that by giving others the chance to drive and lead, he would need to sit in the passenger seat and, for lack of a better phrase, shut up for a while. He would still be able to jerk the steering wheel as needed if disaster were about to strike, but otherwise, he needed to appear cool and confident as they learned the mechanics of it all. Driving a car is all about feeling and intuition, and leadership is no different. The leaders-in-training will never trust themselves if James doesn't allow them to find a groove and confidence in their abilities.

James follows a 6:1 rule religiously. He never allows one person to lead more than six people. This forces micro teams to develop within his mega team. He also knows leadership is a crockpot, just like Emma is learning now. It takes 18 months or longer to fully develop a solid leader. He provides regular and intentional time, attention, and feedback to those leaders during that incubation period. He shows up with empathy and open communication to foster the most positive environment he can. He leads his own micro team on the production side while also leading and growing others.

Emma is following that example. With Erik's coaching, she transitions her team out of the messy middle. She builds micro teams within her mega team. When an agent starts excelling, they can then move to Tier 5 and hire a partner as well, thus repeating the process and scaling leadership. Emma continues to strengthen her emotional intelligence and empathy through the works of great authors like Brene Brown and Adam Grant. She allows her leaders to lead and steps more and more into a mentorship role.

When she runs into Trevor again at the next Hatch Coaching Summit the following year, she knows she needs to be honest with him about their conversation the previous fall. They decide to grab breakfast at a coffee shop downtown. Emma discloses to Trevor that despite the arrogance she wore as a mask last year, she was really struggling.

"I wasn't sure where I wanted to go with the future of my business, and I was pretty dishonest with you," she shares. "I remember talking big about what was going on for me, but I was so lost. I wish I could have been vulnerable, but it was too hard at the time. I really regret that. I'm sorry."

Trevor is grateful for Emma's honesty, even if it came a year later. He shares with her how that conversation wasn't a regret for him at all because it really led him to dig deep about what it was he wanted. Envying what looked so convincingly like greener grass on her side of the fence, Trevor realized there were patches of his own yard that he needed to be watering instead.

Trevor now sees he never wanted to grow bigger; he wanted to grow stronger. He examined his team closely and decided to stay a micro team. He reminds himself often of something he heard from Erik Hatch at the Summit, "Real estate is easy. People are difficult." It was clear to Trevor as the Summit wrapped up that a showing partner on his team had Empire Builder material written all over him. Upon returning home, he immediately set into motion the process of building that person up. Over the last year, he's seen how that decision helped the business flourish. Trevor now knows he never really wanted out of production completely; he just wanted to make sure he had a strong and mighty team alongside him.

COMMON TIER 7 PAIN POINTS:

As a full-time leader and full-time producer, time for a Tier 7 leader is stretched thin. As we saw in the examples of Trevor, Emma, and James, it's possible for a business to grow in many different directions. It's more crucial than ever before that a Tier 7 leader be self-aware, reflective, and intentional so the vision of the company can be clearly communicated to the team. People yearn for clarity, and if the leader is unclear, the team is at risk of falling apart.

Another common pain point of Tier 7 is the pressure of carrying all of the major leadership duties alone. A rainmaker in this stage is still the channel through which decision making flows, so despite having given some responsibility to others, those people do not yet have authority to go along with it. Decision-making power for the big stuff still rests on the rainmaker's shoulders. The rainmaker is the one to vision cast and see the opportunities the business is providing, and it's natural to wonder if there is a better way to capitalize on the momentum. There's a lot of questions but not a lot of time to sit and think about them.

It's an important time to focus on building up the other leaders on the team, even hiring externally if needed. The story of James in the previous section emphasizes the importance of allowing the newbie leader to learn to drive without the undue pressure and stress of being micromanaged. A major hurdle for many rainmakers in this stage is the desire to metaphorically grab the wheel from the newbie-in-training when they see a danger on the road ahead. It's tempting to try to save people from discomfort, but in doing so, they're also robbed of an opportunity to learn from it and repair the damage. It's important to allow people to fail. The biggest growth happens right afterwards.

The final pain point for those leaders who want to stay a micro team is a double-edged one. A byproduct of awesomeness is business will continue to grow. Delivering a high level of service will continue to attract people, and a leader will sometimes need to make the conscious decision to let some opportunities go, not only for themselves but also for their team. For that reason, excellence truly is a threat to staying small.

HATCH HINT

The Threat

When you deliver a high level of service, growth will find you. If you desire to stay "small," you will have to consciously let go of some opportunities for you and for those you serve.

Excellence is a threat to staying small.

HATCH MODEL INSIGHT: TIER 7

Erik: Bigger and better aren't synonyms. The key word here is **progression**. Contentment, satisfaction, and joy don't always come from a huge life. They come from moving the ball forward. *Do I know more than I did yesterday? Did I inch myself/this cause/this business forward toward a goal I believe in? Did I learn from my mistakes and pivot in the ways needed to make progress tomorrow?* Each one of us is going to have a different set of goals, values, and ideas of what we want our lives to look like. In order to choose the path that's right for you, get very clear on your own wants.

What Makes You Happy?

The greatest joy that exists is the feeling of progression. It leads to a feeling of self worth and increases job satisfaction.

"Progress is happiness." - Tony Robbins

In his book *The Motive*, Patrick Lencioni writes that leaders choose leadership because they are either motivated by a passion to serve others or a passion to be rewarded. Additionally, I would argue that in order to be an effective CEO, you need to be called to lead. I've known many people throughout my career who have wanted to make as much as possible and work as little as possible. Lofty stuff. But surprisingly, mega teams aren't necessarily the way to get that.

If you are going to choose the mega team route, you need to love the following:

1. Developing a leadership team
2. Managing team members
3. Having difficult conversations
4. Running great team meetings
5. Communicating constantly with team members

Take a look at that list. It's not full of transactions or data points. Every single item has to do with people. As the CEO of a mega team, you will be **people-ing** all day, every day for the sheer fact that you have so many people within your ecosystem. At any given moment, someone on the team is going to have an issue with a team member. Someone is going to need encouragement. Someone is going to need constructive feedback. Your job as the leader of many individuals might as well be called the CRO - Chief Repeating Officer. It's believed that people need to hear something upwards of seven times before they remember it.

There is a concept called **the Rule of 3s and 10s** that is incredibly helpful in thinking about leadership and the need to continually adjust the sails. Each and every time an organization hits a three or 10 milestone (3 people, 10 people, 30 people, 100 people, etc.), things need to change. Leadership structure, meetings, standard operating procedures – all of it will need to be fine tuned to meet the needs of the team.

The Rule of 3s and 10s

When an organization hits 3 team members, 10 team members, 30 team members, 100 team members, etc. (the multiple continues) - the entire ecosystem changes. Organization charts shift, new leaders are developed, and massive new challenges arise.

As an example, people hit a glass ceiling with 10-15 people. They see where they want to get to, but it just never seems to happen. It isn't until the leader starts thinking and operating like a leader of 30 that the team will make healthy strides toward growth.

Leadership matters.

A team made up of three to 10 people is the most powerful, nimble, profitable, and well-oiled with a great deal of proximity and little flight risk. When you grow past 10 people, choosing to go medium or mega, you are now creating leadership issues that weren't there before. That's a ceiling a lot of people hit. They get to 15 people and don't know why they're not getting the same results. They didn't adjust their sails. They stayed the same while their entire organization changed. This is why it's crucial for a leader to be 12 months ahead on vision casting and six months ahead on hiring.

Work Ahead

- Erik recommends being at least 12 months ahead on vision casting and at least six months ahead on hiring.
- Your job as the leader is to see where you are going and get people onboard. Casting the vision and winning the room over takes time and intentionality.
- Additionally, if you need a hire to join your ecosystem, you need to be proactive with that with a 6-month runway. You have to place the ad, go through the interview process, oftentimes get them licensed, and then get them trained before they ever make a difference in your ecosystem.

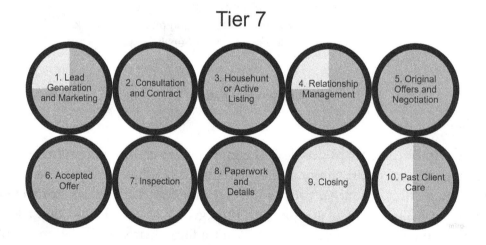

TIER 7 : "The micro-team is rocking. Stay micro, grow to medium, or reach for mega?"

Production #s: 100+ transactions

Team size: 6+

CEO Salary: $30,000+

Where should you focus your time?
- More time spent on leadership & business development rather than production
- 1-on-1s
- Vision casting
- Hiring/recruiting
- Community engagement
- Coaching + Training
- Management
- If you have an Empire Builder for your micro team, your energy with clients is simply that of a Chief Relationship Officer (CRO)

Pain Points:
- Full-time leader + full-time producer
- Time is stretched massively
- Everything is now customized
- You are wearing too many hats
- New team members are needing a plethora of training & that falls on you
- You are the channel in which decisions flow through, and although you've given people responsibility, they don't yet have authority. You see the opportunities your business is providing, and you can't help but wonder if there is a better way to capitalize on the momentum you have

Solution:
- You can't do it alone. Raising up leaders from within (or hiring externally) is the next step
- Production & retention will be unpredictable if you don't concentrate on great leadership from others, so you start empowering key people with great character
- Your business model(s) continue to progress and your time is invested into creating future opportunities for you and your team to grow

New Tools Needed: None

Graduation Checklist:
- Agents performing at or above standard
- Each department has a rhythm with high levels of competency, micro teams are developing
- 4+ months of business & personal expenses in the bank
- Profit numbers are at a green light

Expected Income (Salary, Production, and Profit):
- Collecting a respectable salary
- Earning 20-25% if you have an Empire Builder on each transaction from your micro team OR earning 30-45% from your personal transactions (while paying the salary of the showing partner from your personal side & possibly 5% of your commission)
- 30-45% from ISA set appointments (while paying 10% to the ISA from your personal commission)
- Agents feeding into a higher GCI will impact your bottom line of getting the business to 25% profit+

Tier 8: Development and Duplication

There is a stark difference between Tiers 7 and 8. In Tier 7, a rainmaker is still responsible for the urgent and the important. In Tier 8, the built-in leaders are now tending to the urgent, and the rainmaker is now focusing on the important. Tiers 8, 9, and 10 all have very little to do with real estate and everything to do with leadership. More specifically, Tier 8 focuses on **development** and **duplication**. Various team members are coached up and slowly, intentionally developed into leaders to serve the team as a whole. Rainmakers develop other legs and arms of the business. Agents duplicate the process and develop their own micro teams. The continual development and duplication allows the team to grow even stronger.

Tier 8 - Mega Team Example

Rainmaker Agent*

*the rainmaker has also likely opened other businesses such as mortgage, title, insurance, property management, home flipping, etc.

- Lead ISA
  - ISA
  - ISA
  - ISA Partner
- Lead Agent
  - Micro Team Lead Agent
    - Agent
    - Empire Builder
      - Showing Partner
    - Agent
    - Agent
    - Agent
    - Agent
    - Agent
  - Micro Team Lead Agent
    - Agent
    - Empire Builder
      - Showing Partner
      - Showing Partner
    - Showing Partner
  - Empire Builder
    - Showing Partner
  - Micro Team Lead Agent
    - Agent
    - Showing Partner
    - Showing Partner
    - Showing Partner
  - Empire Builder
    - Showing Partner
    - Showing Partner
- Lead Admin
  - Admin
  - Admin
    - Admin
  - Admin
    - Admin
  - Admin

DEVELOP AND DUPLICATE

In Tier 8, it's common for teams to be full of talented agents with a desire to grow and evolve. But if the rainmaker hasn't evolved and grown at an even faster rate, those talented agents are a major flight risk. Liz saw this over the past year with her team in the Northeast. One by one, several of her top producing agents left the team to venture off on their own. She struggled immensely watching her once strong and mighty team deflate before her eyes.

Liz knew she needed to look inward to discover how to improve as a leader. She started focusing heavily on self-reflection during her morning routine and gained new awareness and insight while doing so. She discovered she's a fixer by nature and believed for a long time that it came from a place of love. But what she's seeing now is that it's not always coming from love after all. It's an attempt to control. Control is not love based. It's fear based.

True leaders allow people to make mistakes. The terms *helicopter* or *lawnmower parent* have been commonplace in the English vernacular for some time now. Helicopter parents hover over their child, ready to swoop down and save them in the face of struggle. Lawnmower parents take it a step further and walk ahead of their child, clearing obstacles out of the way before the kid even gets to them.

These two concepts apply to business leadership too. Helicopter leaders micromanage their team. Lawnmower leaders step in and resolve issues before the team member has the opportunity to learn anything from them. Neither of these leadership styles allows the necessary space or opportunity for people to mess up.

Growth requires resistance. People don't get stronger on their best days. They get stronger on their hardest days when they've fallen hard and are faced with the choice to stay down or get up again. By micromanaging and problem solving for people instead of **alongside people**, leaders are robbing their team of an opportunity to grow. It may seem well intentioned, but ultimately, it's selfish.

Liz now understands that the agents leaving her team didn't feel loved and supported by her micromanagement. They felt controlled. They didn't see her grab the wheel of the car and think, *She cares so much that she won't let me fail.* Instead, the message was clear. *She wants to be successful now more than she wants me to grow into the person I'm supposed to be tomorrow.* That's not strong leadership.

Strong leadership demands that Liz allows those developing leaders to sit at the wheel of the driver's ed car now, and she needs to slide over to the passenger seat. Instead of grabbing the steering wheel or slamming on the brakes when she senses trouble, Liz needs to sit next to them as they learn to navigate that bumpy path on their own. She's there to offer suggestions or assess what points they need to talk about later, but she's no longer in control of that journey. The leader in training is.

Strong leadership is slow, intentional, and painful, but Liz is ready to take the steps necessary to becoming a strong leader. She continues her self-reflection practices every morning, keeping a pulse on her own strengths and weaknesses to continue to improve herself and her business. She started focusing on the development of other leaders on her team. She takes her time with them, knowing this process can be a couple of years or more while bit by bit instilling in them the faith and trust that will ripen into true autonomy within those leaders over time.

COMMON TIER 8 PAIN POINTS:

Tier 8 is emotionally taxing for many rainmakers because they have long identified as the key person, the filter through which decisions are made. Now in Tier 8, they're moving from that hands-on, day-to-day parent role into more of a grandparenting role. The transition is very often a difficult one, both for the rainmaker and others on the team.

Doubt and resentment have fertile ground in Tier 8 if communication isn't handled properly. Team members who were used to reporting to a 9- or 10-skill-level leader are now being asked to report to a new leader who may only be at a 6- or 7-skill level. To add fuel to the fire for some, the new leader isn't necessarily the person who has been there the longest or the highest producing, but the person who is most built to lead. Resistance to that idea seems like a natural reaction when the vision and purpose is not properly communicated.

Another common pain point in Tier 8 directly related to that resistance is the tendency of the rainmaker to fall into the role of middleman or middlewoman. Let's take Beth, a longstanding admin on Liz's team, as an example. Beth has served as Liz's right-hand lady from the start. She's been on this ride through all of the ups and downs and looks to Liz for leadership. That's been the norm. That's what she's used to. But now Beth is being asked to report to Trisha instead of Liz. Trisha was hired years after her, so Beth is struggling to see Trisha as a supervisor of any kind. When Beth has an issue with something, she continues to view Trisha as a colleague, not an authority figure or leader. She goes to Liz instead. That's what she knows. Over and over again, she breaks the chain of command because she's not bought into the chain of command.

Liz needs to be thorough and intentional about how she communicates the leadership changes to her team to avoid being put in the middle. One very empowering way to do this is to recruit the help of the person being "handed off" to the next leader.

Liz can go to Beth and explain this new chain of command. She can ask for her help, bringing her in and helping her see the why behind it all. She can be authentic with Beth, explaining that handing off those responsibilities is hard for everyone, and she can ask for Beth's patience and understanding through the awkwardness that comes with transitions like that. Liz can set an expectation low and then recruit Beth to provide feedback and insight into how Trisha is doing and how she could continue to improve as a leader.

This creates an increased level of buy-in which is crucial for everyone. The message needs to be communicated that **what was is not what's going to be**. What has been is not the future anymore. There is a new normal. Management by Liz may have worked up until this point, but it's not enough anymore. A mega team requires micro-leadership amongst departments, and the team needs to buy into that for it to work. This message will need to be stated and restated many times before it sinks in, but stay the course and keep it clear.

HATCH MODEL INSIGHT: TIER 8

Erik: Development and duplication can take many forms in Tier 8 – the development of micro teams for agents, the duplication of the model for those micro teams to flourish, developing people as leaders, and developing other arms and legs of the business. To minimize flight risks, an emphasis on development and duplication within the business ecosystem is key.

It's crucial for the rainmaker to be the most dedicated, forward-thinking, and evolutionary member of the team. The focus is no longer working the business; it's **working on the business.** Leadership development and vision casting remain at the forefront of the rainmaker's responsibilities.

True leadership is more of an art than a science. It's hard to quantify because so much of it relies on a feeling. They are willing to take none of the credit but all of the blame. Leaders can readily see the problems, but they don't complain about the problems. They step up to help solve them. They coach people up when needed and coach them out when needed. They are a teacher at heart.

People can often think back and easily remember their favorite teacher. I want you to do that now. Imagine that teacher in your mind. Now, I bet it wasn't the easiest teacher you had, the one that let you slide by with half-assed work. And I bet it wasn't the hard-ass either, the one that got on your case for every misstep. That favorite teacher is usually the one who found that sweet spot balance between what challenged you to learn while also encouraging you to stretch yourself and grow. They truly saw you for you, and they trusted you. I bet you can remember how it felt to be in that classroom where you were valued and appreciated in that way.

Strong leadership is no different. A true leader knows people want to feel trusted. They know their team will make mistakes, no doubt about it, but they will be supported and encouraged as they get back up, knowing that person is going to do better next time because of it. As with many of the tiers before, this process of coaching up new leaders is a **watch me, watch you, go and do process.** Those leaders in training serve on an advisory board while they learn. A strong leader doesn't wait until someone is 100% ready to lead before they hand off the baton. They are able to identify when someone is at a six or seven of a 10-point scale of leadership ability and relinquish enough control to allow that person to grow by doing.

It is around this stage in the business that some rainmakers explore the idea of a sales manager. This is a hire we would advise against. A sales manager will likely cost upwards of 70-100k, and the team often resents this person. They come in and attempt to manage people they don't know. An outside perspective can be incredibly valuable for some things, but this isn't the role for that. Trust is crucial when attempting to hold people accountable, and this person would be coming in with no trust built and no credibility earned. Instead of planting a big tree in the soil of your ecosystem, allow mini teams to grow up from the strong roots that are already established.

Those built-in leaders are coached up in such a way that they are now able to duplicate the process of building a team. Agents on your team duplicate the model, starting at Tier 5 with the hiring of a showing partner. Leaders are appointed to each department so they have that same, close knit mini team of their own. The leaders are not necessarily the longest standing or highest producing, but the person most built to lead. It's crucial to keep things manageable and have no more than five or six people reporting to one person. Raise up decision-makers whenever possible; give people authority.

Appointing those leaders and decision-makers frees up time for the rainmaker. There are less team meetings to attend, fewer moments of someone popping their head in to ask, *"Hey do you have a minute?"* The rainmaker has more time for vision casting and advancement of the business. With new found time and mental capacity, a rainmaker can now start developing other streams of business. This relies heavily on customization and knowledge of what would work best in your particular market but can include a wide range of possibilities, including but not limited to investment properties, mortgage or title companies, coaching, home flipping, handyman/handywoman services, moving companies, or property management.

When your key players are owning those roles and responsibilities without feeling the need to constantly check in with the rainmaker and are no longer seeking the rainmaker's blessing to make a big decision, they have stepped into complete accountability and leadership. That's a beautiful thing for the entire ecosystem, and it's a natural transition to Tier 9.

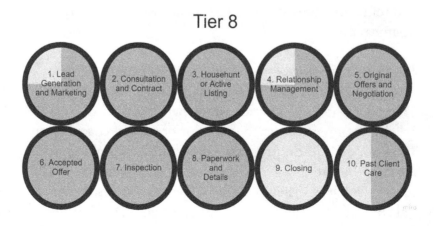

Tier 8

TIER 8 : "Develop and Duplicate"

Production #s: 150+ transactions

Team size: 10+

CEO Salary: $40,000+

Where should you focus your time?

- Time spend on leadership + business development
- You have weekly leadership meetings as well as 1-on-1s with all your emerging leaders
- Look to add arms to your business
- Vision casting
- Hiring/recruiting
- Community engagement
- Coaching + training
- Management
- Your Empire Builder is running the transactions of your micro team so you can serve as CRO to your clients

Pain Points:

- Much of your time is spent on leading your larger team and your micro team
- Day-to-day operations are in full swing, yet there's still so much that flows through you
- You're "the guy" for most everything & that's starting to wear on you
- You recognize decisions should be trusted in the hands of your key leaders & you're the bottleneck

Solution:

- It's time you start to stay in your lane
- If you're going to be a true CEO, you need to wear less hats
- For those hats you do wear, serve those with much more intention
- Trust your people…let them fail so they can learn resiliency and tenacity at a new level

New Tools Needed: None

Graduation Checklist:

- The real estate team is functioning well, you are handing off both responsibility and authority to other leaders, agents are performing at or above standard
- Each department has a rhythm with high levels of competency
- 4+ months of business & personal expenses in the bank
- Profit numbers are at a green light

Expected Income (Salary, Production, and Profit):

- Collecting a respectable salary
- Earning 20-25% if you have an Empire Builder on each transaction from your micro team OR earning 30-45% from your personal transactions (while paying the salary of the partner from your personal side & possibly 5% of your commission)
- 30-45% from ISA set appointments (while paying 10% to the ISA from your personal commission)
- Agents feeding into a higher GCI that will impact your bottom line of getting the business to 25% profit + Earning income from your newly added ancillary businesses

Tier 9: Mastering the C-Suite

The Hatch Model is a **blueprint**, a design plan that can be followed for incredible results. Below you will see an example of a mega team, specifically the Hatch Team. It is a flow-chart of our actual team makeup at the time this book is being written. But as a leader grows into these top tiers of growth, it is more important than ever to get very clear on personal strengths and weaknesses in order to make smart and healthy decisions to support the strength and longevity of the business. For that reason, this blueprint is **customizable,** and it is essential that a leader tailors this plan to his or her specific business in order to reap the best results.

THE PERFECT REAL ESTATE AGENT BLUEPRINT

Tier 9- Mega Team Example

- Rainmaker Agent
  - Lead ISA
    - ISA
    - ISA
    - ISA Partner
  - Lead Agent
    - Micro Team Lead Agent
      - Agent
      - Empire Builder
        - Showing Partner
      - Agent
      - Agent
      - Agent
      - Agent
      - Agent
      - Agent
    - Micro Team Lead Agent
      - Agent
      - Empire Builder
        - Showing Partner
        - Showing Partner
      - Agent
      - Showing Partner
    - Empire Builder
      - Showing Partner
    - Micro Team Lead Agent
      - Agent
        - Showing Partner
      - Showing Partner
        - Showing Partner
    - Empire Builder
      - Showing Partner
      - Showing Partner
  - Lead Admin
    - Admin
    - Admin
      - Admin
    - Admin
      - Admin
    - Admin

MASTERING THE C-SUITE

Maria is a realtor in the Southwest. She's built a booming business, leaning into her gregarious, larger-than-life personality and her ability to keep dreaming big for herself and her business. She's built a strong and loyal mega team and knows in order to keep her business healthy, she needs to build a solid C-Suite to leverage her weaknesses.

The C-Suite titles and responsibilities differ from industry to industry. Within any given business or organization, there can be a wide range of C-Suite Executives - a Chief Executing Officer (CEO), Chief Financial Officer (CFO), Chief Marketing Officer (CMO), Chief Technology Officer (CTO), COO (Chief Operations Officer), and CHRO (Chief Human Resources Officer), just to name a few.

Maria knows she needs to create a balanced C-Suite. It's not necessary for her to build a lengthy list of executives in that suite, but it needs to be comprehensive enough to foster a healthy, sustainable team. The key roles she needs to consider are Chief Executing Officer (CEO), Chief Operations Officer (COO), and something we in the Hatch Model call the Chief Culture Officer (CCO). Maria has been leading as CEO throughout her team's growth thus far. She has been vision casting, guiding the team, coaching up individuals as needed, and creating the kind of organization that will continue to grow and thrive. She loves it, and her strengths support it. She's built to be a CEO.

The Main Responsibilities of a CEO:
1. Cast the vision
2. Lead the leaders
3. Coach

But her rainmaker buddy Malik in a neighboring community doesn't have the same skill set. He's been in the game about as long as Maria, and he's also built a successful team. Interestingly, he's done so with a nearly opposite set of strengths. Maria is a cheerleader and a dreamer; Malik is conscientious and strategic. He loves coaching people up but does so with strategic goal setting and analysis. He's a problem solver, a clear communicator, and a diligent leader. He's not designed for the CEO role, but he's a master of operations. He is still very capable of sitting at the head of the table, but he's doing so from the COO chair.

Maria and Malik are both great leaders. They're encouraging, forward thinking, and action oriented, but they are fundamentally very different people with very different strengths. Maria will lead her team as the rainmaker with the title of CEO, and Malik will lead his with the title of COO. Maria will look for a detail- and data-oriented problem solver to fill the COO position on her team. Malik will look for an optimistic, enthusiastic innovator to fill the CEO position on his team. Neither CEO or COO is better than the other in terms of leadership. Much like the two initial admin hires in Tiers 2 and 3, these positions should complement each other and converge to make a solid leadership pair.

The quickest way for Maria to find this COO counterpart is for her to promote from within her own ecosystem. The person should be known, liked, trusted, and have a remarkable competency in her business. The other choice, which will take longer but can be equally fruitful, is to make a recruitment play. She could seek four or five respected leaders from the community to let them know she's interested in them joining the team. There's no best choice here, no one-size-fits-all method to go about hiring this person, but she should most definitely seek coaching and guidance to help with the process. This role is crucial and needs a second or even third set of eyes on it to make a sound choice. A coach can help clearly identify who Maria is looking for, the right compensation programs, the hiring process that will bring forth the best results, and help cast a wide net to make sure Maria makes a logical choice that will help her business thrive.

Once that hire is made, the final spot to fill in this C-Suite executive team is to find a Chief Culture Officer (CCO). This is the person who keeps a pulse on what is happening on the team. The CCO will be a champion for each individual on the team. They celebrate in the good - birthdays, pregnancy announcements, engagements, career milestones, and retirements. They also show up in the pain - the loss of a loved one, a family member in the hospital, and major life disappointments. They organize meal trains, send flowers, and deliver gifts.

But it's also important that they show up in the mundane. They are responsible for creating moments of connection for the team, being emotionally available, and taking sincere interest in the lives of their colleagues. This person is a galvanizer, a cheerleader for those around them. In some ways, this person is similar to the role of a human relations specialist, helping with recruitment efforts as needed and working to resolve interpersonal conflicts among team members.

COMMON TIER 9 PAIN POINTS:

CEOs and COOs need to get out of their own way and accept the help they need both for themselves and the future of their business. The rainmaker, the founding leader of the company, may be tempted to argue that since they built the company into what it is so far, it qualifies them to continue building it into the future. But the company may have quadrupled (or more) in size over the last few years, and it is ignorant and shortsighted to assume they can continue to carry the C-Suite responsibilities alone. It's too much for any individual to do solo.

A great CEO or COO also needs to be open to constructive criticism, relying heavily on trusted advisors and colleagues to provide honest feedback on their leadership as the company grows. Every leader has blind spots, and if they're not open to listening to different perspectives, the company is vulnerable to disasters. A diligent practice of self-assessment and reflection needs to be a habit for any C-Suite executive. *What am I doing well? What do I need to work on? How will I improve?*

HATCH MODEL INSIGHT: TIER 9

Erik: I serve as the CEO at Hatch Realty and Hatch Coaching. I am the vision caster and head coach, leading the leaders of the team. I bring credibility and attention to the business by being an involved and recognizable figure in the community. I serve on boards, work with nonprofits, and keep a trustworthy reputation. I am the public-facing Hatch mascot in the Fargo community. The mascot may not play in the game, but it represents the team. That's my job.

Although leadership has always been a strength for me, the CEO role is one I had to grow into over time. Two of the most persistent hurdles that have popped up again and again have been relationship management and clear, consistent boundaries. As we discussed in the previous section, helicopter and lawnmower leadership styles are common tendencies a leader can fall into. But they are also shortsighted and ultimately selfish on the part of the leader. Instead, the C-Suite should serve as first responders; they don't prevent the accidents from happening, but they are right there to provide assistance when one does.

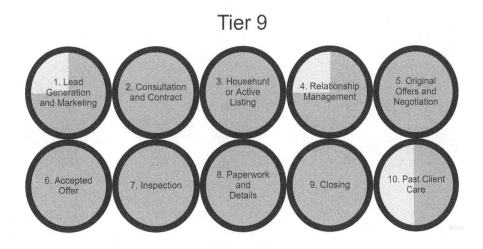

TIER 9 : "Master the CEO role"

Production #s: 200+ transactions

Team size: 15+

CEO Salary: $70,000+

Where should you focus your time?
- Vision cast
- Lead the leaders
- Coach
- That's it. You're the CRO for your micro team

Pain Points:
- Boredom starts to set in. You love to build things, & you've now created an ecosystem that takes care of itself
- You watch decisions being made that you don't necessarily agree with, but you know that your team needs to learn by trial & error & not by you grabbing the steering wheel from them
- You have leveraged most of the day-to-day operations & your development of other leaders is your new glass ceiling

Solution:
- Finding & developing your replacement(s) will take time
- They need to earn the right to be trusted by both you & the organization
- If you want out, the only way is through incredible leadership

New Tools Needed: None

Graduation Checklist:
- A new CEO is identified and developed
- The team is high achieving & is being led exceedingly well by your key leaders
- Agents are performing at or above standard
- 4+ months of business expenses in the bank
- Profit numbers are at a green light

Expected Income (Salary, Production, and Profit):
- Collecting a substantial salary
- Earning 20-25% if you have an Empire Builder on each transaction from your micro team OR earning 30-45% from your personal transactions (while paying the salary of the partner from your personal side and possibly 5% of your commission)
- 30-45% from ISA set appointments (while paying 10% to the ISA from your personal commission)
- Agents feeding into a higher GCI that will impact your bottom line of getting the business to 25% profit +
- Earning income from your newly added ancillary businesses

Tier 10: Stepping Away

Tier 10 is when a leader can stop moving the goalposts. Leaders feel empowered. Solid systems, processes, and branches of the business have been established and are running smoothly. CEOs, like Joy who we meet in this Tier, can decide for themselves what is in their best interest. Do they have more to give this team, or is it time to allow others to take the reins?

THE HATCH MODEL BLUEPRINT

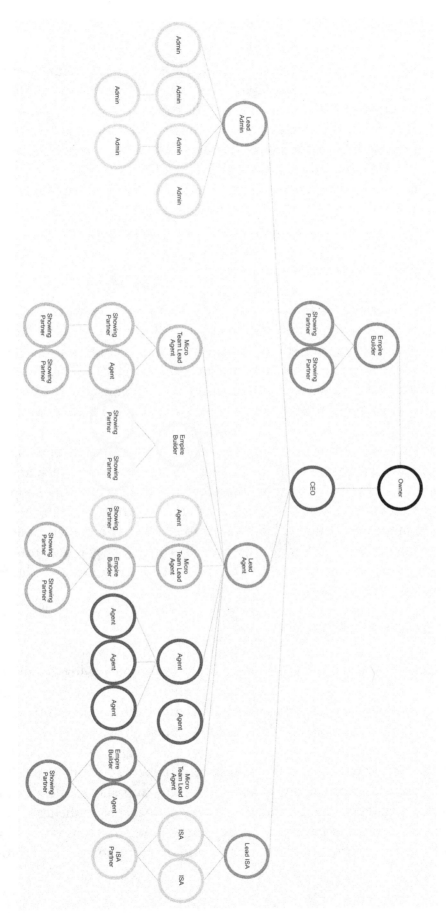

Tier 10- Mega Team Example

111

OWNER ONLY

Joy is a rainmaker and CEO of a mega team in the Midwest. With a carefully curated team of superstars by her side, she's built a company with a strong foundation, stacked bench, and the fortitude to withstand almost any storm. She's sank, she's swam, she's stumbled, and she's soared. She's worked in the industry for nearly two decades and feels her heart being pulled toward other interests and pursuits. She would love to spend more time traveling with family and investing time and energy in the offshoots of the business that are gaining traction, namely coaching and property investment. She looks around at her team and sees a very capable COO, CCO, and a well-trusted agent on the team who has the skills needed to take over as the CEO if given the opportunity. She feels both pride and anxiety about this moment. She could walk away from everything she's worked so hard to build. It would be okay. Her team would be okay.

In order to know with certainty that the team is ready for Joy to step back from the business and relinquish control, all roles she currently occupies will need to be filled. A clear hand off needs to happen either by hiring someone from within or recruiting from the outside. This is done over a long period of time and with great intentionality. Proximity and trust are absolutely crucial to the health of the team, and those relationships are earned. It can take months and months, if not years, to transition that power in a healthy way.

Once all necessary seats are filled, Joy can run a pressure test of sorts. She will need to take 28 days off to see what happens in her absence. Now as the leader, we know this is no easy assignment, but this practice run is absolutely necessary to see what happens. This means no emails, no phone calls, and no quick check-ins. Joy truly needs to check out for a month. A strong and healthy team will know how to patch the holes that come up while she is away. But if there seems to be fire after fire? That means they're not ready. And if that's the case, Joy can use those fires as data to know where she needs to be building up leaders and providing more support.

COMMON TIER 10 PAIN POINTS:

The greatest pain point in Tier 10 is often the ego of the team leader. Moving out of leadership can be really tough. It can be awkward. It can be messy. It can be full of big emotions. It is not uncommon for people to leave when this transition of leadership is happening because the fear of the unknown can push people to jump ship.

For the health and vitality of the team, it's crucial to cast the vision long before the transition happens. Plant the seed that this change is coming, and allow time and space for questions, processing, and eventual acceptance. Ask big influencers on the team to take an active role in the transition and have their fingerprints all over it. Transparency increases buy-in, and that buy-in, in turn, leads to a stronger and more supportive team throughout the transition.

HATCH MODEL INSIGHT: TIER 10

Erik: Once a CEO like Joy hands off leadership and steps away from the business, she will very likely serve on the board (literal or figurative). However, what she does with the rest of her time is up to her. Some leaders simply retire. Others replace that passion with something new to build. It's rare that person slows down unless they're entering into a totally new season of life.

I am not into Tier 10 yet myself because I know I have more to give at Hatch Realty. I reflect back on this whole journey with a smile. I've climbed these tiers, and I've played a lot of parts along the way. The naive part timer trying to scrap his way out of financial trouble, his heart still set on youth ministry. A cocky young realtor, kicked out of his first brokerage when he flew too close to the sun and lost sight of what mattered. A determined agent with a fresh start, hellbent on doing things right. A leader of a growing team, trying to balance it all. And now, a CEO and coach, knowing that I'm approaching Tier 10. I'm not quite ready to step away from the bustling business I fought so hard for, but I can see they have what they need to make it work if I did.

Tier 10 is like a parent watching their kid drive away to college. There is pride, of course, but also grief. "They don't need me anymore" can feel like both a victory and a loss. Let that be okay. It can be both. You can watch them drive away and know you did a good job.

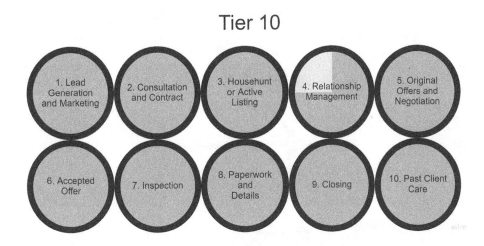

TIER 10 : "Own the business only"

Production #s: 200+ transactions

Team size: 15+

CEO Salary: $70,000+

Where should you focus your time?
- You are completely out of the day-to-day operations of the team
- Your only involvement would be meetings with your CEO & then serving as the CRO for your micro team

Pain Points:
- Your business completely runs itself, & you have a lot of time and money on your hands
- Without purpose or intention with these resources, a lack of fulfillment is inevitable

Solution:
- Find your next challenge or adventure & start putting your passion and wealth to work

New Tools Needed: None

Graduation Checklist: None

Expected Income (Salary, Production, and Profit):
- No salary
- Earning 20-25% from your micro team transactions (led by your Empire Builder)
- Agents feeding into a higher GCI that will impact your bottom line of getting the business to 25% profit +
- Consistent income from your ancillary businesses

Conclusion

Education without implementation is merely entertainment. So, take action toward building the perfect real estate business with this blueprint! Don't hesitate. Go. Now. Make a move!

References

Mandolesi, Laura et al. "Effects of Physical Exercise on Cognitive Functioning and Wellbeing:

Biological and Psychological Benefits." Frontiers in psychology vol. 9 509. 27 Apr. 2018,

doi:10.3389/fpsyg.2018.00509

Sahakian, B. J. & Labuzetta, J. N. (2013). Bad moves: how decision making goes wrong, and the ethics of smart drugs. London: Oxford University Press.

CPSIA information can be obtained
at www.ICGtesting.com
Printed in the USA
BVHW061615180722
641902BV00006B/27